EX UNO PLURES
Traditional Southern Presbyterian Thought on Race Relations

A Symposium With Contributions By
John B. Adger   James Henley Thornwell
R. S. Breck   E. T. Baird   Benjamin M. Palmer
Robert Lewis Dabney   L. Nelson Bell   B. W. Crouch
William A. Plecker   William H. Frazer
J. David Simpson   J. E. Flow
Morton H. Smith   Guy T. Gillespie

Introduction By
Greg Loren Durand, editor

Institute for Southern Historical Review
Toccoa, Georgia

Ex Uno Plures:
Traditional Southern Presbyterian Thought on Race Relations
Greg Loren Durand, editor

Published by
Institute for Southern Historical Review
Post Office Box 2027
Toccoa, Georgia 30577
www.southernhistoricalreview.org

cover and interior by
Magnolia Graphic Design
www.magnoliagraphicdesign.com

Typeset in Palatino Linotype

ISBN-13: 978-0692543283
ISBN-10: 0692543287

God that made the world and all things therein, seeing that he is Lord of heaven and earth, dwelleth not in temples made with hands; neither is worshipped with men's hands, as though he needed any thing, seeing he giveth to all life, and breath, and all things; *and hath made of one blood all nations of men for to dwell on all the face of the earth, and hath determined the times before appointed, and the bounds of their habitation;* that they should seek the Lord, if haply they might feel after him, and find him, though he be not far from every one of us: for in him we live, and move, and have our being; as certain also of your own poets have said, For we are also his offspring.

– Acts 17:24-28

God that made the world and all things
therein, seeing that he is Lord of heaven and earth,
dwelleth not in temples made with hands; Neither
is worshipped with men's hands, as though he
needeth any thing, seeing he giveth to all life, and
breath, and all things; ...that they should seek
the Lord, if haply they might feel after him, and
find him, though he be not far from every one of us:
For in him we live, and move, and have our being;
...as certain also of your own poets have said, For we
are also his offspring.

Acts 17: 24-28

CONTENTS

PART ONE:
NINETEENTH CENTURY

PART TWO:
TWENTIETH CENTURY

INTRODUCTION
by Greg Loren Durand

At the recent 43rd General Assembly of the Presbyterian Church of America (PCA), held from June 9-12, 2015 in Chattanooga, Tennessee, there was, following nine hours of intense discussion, what was touted as a spontaneous moving of the Holy Spirit. Attendees spent the final hour of the Assembly in tearful prayer for racial reconciliation and repentance for the past sins of Southern Presbyterianism, of which the PCA is the direct descendent. In a resolution presented by J. Ligon Duncan and Sean Lucas, both ministers in Mississippi churches, the Assembly was urged to "confess our complicity and involvement in racial injustice during the Civil Rights era up until the present day" – this despite the fact that the PCA did not even exist as a denomination until 1973 and the majority of the men in attendance at the Assembly were either not yet born, or were too young to have participated in such "racial injustice." While no official confession resulted from the debates, scores of ministers dutifully lined up to sign a protestation of the delay, repenting to one another of their latent "racism," especially to fellow ministers of African descent.

Of course, this "White guilt" did not originate just fifty

years ago with opposition to the Civil Rights movement, but, according to the resolution adopted in 2002 by the 30th General Assembly of the PCA, and the 2004 "Pastoral Letter on Racism" drafted by a committee of the 32nd General Assembly, it should also be extended back into the antebellum period to include the "oppression, racism, exploitation, manstealing, and chattel slavery" allegedly defended and perpetrated by Southern Presbyterianism in general, and specifically by leaders such as Robert Lewis Dabney of Virginia, James Henley Thornwell of South Carolina, and Benjamin Morgan Palmer of Louisiana. The unspoken assumption here, of course, is that the present generation is more enlightened than, and thus in a tenable position to pass judgment on, those of the past. We Christians in the Twenty-First Century are advantaged in having the social justice of *Brown v. Board of Education*, the transcendent wisdom of Dr. Martin Luther King, and the speechcraft of modern hucksters of ethnic neuroses to raise our consciousness above the thick-headed backwardness of our neanderthalic forebears.

However, with very few exceptions, there is no one in the Presbyterian world today – the PCA included – who is qualified to even stand in the shadow of such men as these. Indeed, they were theological giants in their time and one is hard-pressed to imagine the likes of them ever walking the earth again. It would behoove the chronically repentant churchian to dispassionately consider the actual words of these great men and perhaps lay aside – to borrow a term from C. S. Lewis – their "chronological snobbery." The progress of time does not necessarily result in the evolutionary advancement of the collective mind of man. Not without good reason, Scripture instructs God's people to disdain innovation and to seek instead the "old paths" (Jer. 6:16).

Furthermore, to attribute the fancies of one's own imagination to the promptings of the Spirit is presumptuous at the very least. Certainly, to claim to be divinely moved to repentance of a sin that is completely unknown in the inspired Scriptures is to plant a dangerous seed which may one day bring forth the fruit of open infidelity. Many of the Abolitionists of the antebellum period demonstrated the truth of this when they began by proclaiming, not just the abuses, but the very institution of African servitude itself as inherently wicked, and ended in the functionally atheistic demand for "an anti-slavery Constitution, an anti-slavery Bible, and an anti-slavery God." When a fervid philanthropy dislodges the authority of God's Word from its rightful throne in the human mind, nothing but a disastrous apostasy will be the result. This is certainly an instance where one's repentance needs to be repented of.

The present volume is divided into two parts. The first part contains the writings of the aforementioned Presbyterian divines – Dabney, Thornwell, and Palmer – as well as contributions from lesser-known clergymen, such as E. T. Baird of Jackson, Mississippi and John B. Adger of Charleston, South Carolina. Like the proverbial drunken uncle at a family reunion, these men are often viewed with a mixture of affection and embarrassment in modern-day Presbyterianism. The "stool of everlasting repentance" will never want of an occupant eager to reconcile his ecclesiastical heritage to the ongoing march of political correctness. Invariably, the former will be sacrificed to the latter when he realizes that tearful ablutions and emotional self-flagellations are impotent to propitiate the gods of imaginary guilt.

On the subject of race relations, the traditional Southern Presbyterian position was indeed what would be considered today controversial. However, it should be remembered that these men lived in a different time and under much different circumstances than those to which we are accustomed. The illustrious John Calvin himself once noted that social and political structures must vary to suit the diverse character and needs of their respective populations. If individual family units differ from each other in mental and moral capacities, it is reasonable to conclude that this diversity is magnified on the larger scale of ethnic groupings of mankind. The form of government best adapted to one race of people cannot be made to conform to another that is entirely dissimilar in thought and behavior.

It is undeniable that the American political system had been carefully designed by its framers with the peculiarities of the White race in mind. Centuries of development of political theory in Europe also played an important role in the formation of our institutions. When Thomas Jefferson penned his famous declaration that "all men are created equal," he did not entertain the delusion that "all men" are equally intended by "nature or nature's God" to live under the same conditions. When the later Constitution was drafted for themselves and their "posterity," it is clear that the framers had the same meaning of the word in mind that the head of a family has when bequeathing his estate to his own offspring in his last will and testament.

Almost without exception, the early Americans viewed the imported natives of the "dark continent" as a foreign element in their midst and legislated accordingly. When slavery was forced upon the colonies by imperial decree, repeated appeals were made to the British crown, by Southerners in particular, to quell the influx of a population that tended to weaken, and would eventually bring disaster upon, White civilization in the New World. Their entreaties ignored, and the presence of the Black race in large numbers an established fact, a well-developed legal and social structure necessarily arose that accorded with the general welfare of the community while affording a level of personal liberty appropriate to the capacity of the individual to make proper use of it.

Only a few generations removed from his native state of barbarism in Africa, the Black man with whom Southerners were acquainted had not the advantage of a century and a half of Yankee "benevolence" and "education." The memory of no less than eighty servile insurrections in the Caribbean, including the wanton rapine and slaughter of Whites during the Haitian uprisings around the turn of the Nineteenth Century, was fresh in the Southern mind. Nor had they forgotten the more recent Denmark Vesey conspiracy in Charleston, South Carolina, or the Nat Turner insurrection at Southampton, Virginia. The benevolent system of Southern slavery had done much to ameliorate the Negro's natural inclination to violence, instilling in its place a familial affection for his White master, and a respect for White society in general; however the rapidity with which so many reverted to savagery during the "fool's errand" of radical Reconstruction, seemed to justify the profound unease wrought within the Southern psyche with regard to absolute Negro equality. Certainly one cannot be condemned for acting upon what he honestly believes, and what experience itself confirms, to be true.

As will be seen in the following pages, the Southern Presbyterian view of race relations was grounded solidly on what has recently become known as the "two kingdom" paradigm. The realms of Church and State – of the redemptive and the common spheres of the divine government – were to be kept distinct and never commingled. Just as the State could not intrude into the jurisdiction of the Church, to dictate in solely ecclesiastical or doctrinal matters, so the Church could not presume to dictate to the State matters of purely political function. In America, the State – more specifically the several States of the South – had declared the Negro unfit for social or political equality with the White man, and had prescribed a system of servitude suited to his nature and conducive to the order and peace of the community. Absent clear biblical condemnation, or reasonably consequent moral arguments drawn from biblical precepts, it was firmly believed that the Church as an institution had no right to declaim any existing institution of the State, but was bound to inculcate in its members a humble submission thereunto. The apostolic instructions of Romans 13:1-7 and 1 Peter 2:13-17 were taken seriously by Southern Christians, even though they were often ignored by fanatical religionists in the North.

However, this natural and institutionalized inequality in the socio-political realm did not carry over to the spiritual realm. Without exception, the leading Southern theologians viewed the Black man as possessive of the same spiritual dignity as the White man, and therefore the same corresponding right to religious instruction and access to the Gospel message. Though the churches were often segregated by race, and Blacks were generally forbidden to hold religious services apart from White oversight, this was done to protect and not harm Black Christians. It was understood that Christianity works a moral change on the soul, but does not necessarily alter one's genetic characteristics. Southerners knew the propensity of the Negro mind to enthusiastic excess, and oversight was deemed necessary to maintain orthodoxy and orthopraxy. At the same time, it was considered detrimental to the White congregations to be hampered by the necessity to tailor instruction to the needs of those at a lower level of religious development. The sermons by R.S. Breck and E.T. Baird included in the present volume will give some insight into the common reasoning behind this practice.

Part Two consists exclusively of shorter papers and editorials which appeared in *The Southern Presbyterian Journal* during the 1940s and 1950s, written by J. David Simpson, Morton H. Smith, Guy T. Gillespie, and others, and covering forced integration, inter-racial marriage, the anti-White agenda of the Civil Rights movement, and other similar matters. It will immediately be noticed that these authors self-consciously followed in the philosophical footsteps of their ecclesiastical predecessors of the previous century, most notably B.M. Palmer. Although their adversary had exchanged the outward trappings of the fanatical Abolitionism of the Nineteenth Century for that of the Cultural Marxism of the Twentieth Century, the content of the persistent attack on traditional Christian values remained precisely the same. These were the very men targeted for criticism by those who instigated the emotional spectacle at the 43rd General Assembly, and leaflets containing extracts from their writings were circulated in an effort to "educate" those who were unfamiliar with the shadowy background of their denomination. Certainly, however, intellectual integrity requires one to read the allegedly incriminating statements in their original context before passing judgment on their authors.

According to an old adage, "It is impossible to unscramble an egg." Just as the institution of African slavery was abolished in this country, never to return, so legal segregation of the races is not likely to ever be re-established in the United States. Whites and Blacks live together, work together, worship together, and even conjugally relate together. The Christian who holds to a providential interpretation of history, must see the hand of God in "whatsoever comes to pass." However, whether or not this new state of things has wrought a blessing or a curse for both the Church and the State, the reader is left to decide for himself.

The intent, however, in bringing the following sermons, essays, and editorials together under one cover is to allow past Southern Presbyterian leaders to be heard in their own defense. The evidence is undeniable that the attitude of Southern Presbyterianism in general was always paternal, and never maliciously discriminatory, toward the Black man. As stated above, they were men who lived at a different time and under different circumstances, and they should be so judged, and not by modern social conditions of which they knew nothing. They professed to be, and all evidence shows them to have been, men of integrity and sincere faith. Above all, these men should be judged by the clear and stedfast testimony of Scripture, and not the ever-changing standard of public opinion. The Savior condensed the moral law down to but two commandments: "Thou shalt love the Lord thy God with all thy heart, and with all thy soul, and with all thy mind.... And thou shalt love thy neighbor as thyself" (Matt. 22:37, 39). If our predecessors cannot be proved to have failed in their duties to God and their fellow men, then we have no alternative but to hold them guiltless.

September, 2015

PART ONE:
NINETEENTH CENTURY

I

The Christian Doctrine of Human Rights and Slavery
by Rev. John B. Adger, D.D.

"The powers that be are ordained of God." Here is the Christian doctrine of the origin of government. Civil polity is not a device of man, but the institution of God; nor is it the result of a compact between the individuals of a multitude, each of whom was previously the sole master of himself. It is rather the offspring of the nature and providential circumstances which God has assigned to man. It is pure fiction to assert that the state of nature ever was a state of individual independence. Mankind from the beginning never have existed otherwise than in society and under government. The principle of subjection to government is not that principle of common honesty which binds a man to his own engagements, nor yet that principle of political honesty which binds the child to his ancestors' engagements; for of all the rightful subjects of government that do now exist, or ever did exist, not one in a million ever yielded his consent, or was ever asked for his consent to any

such compact. The principle of subjection to government
is a conscientious submission to the will of God. The Creator originally destined man for society and civilization.
These, and not barbarism and personal savage independence, are his natural state.[1] And consequently, all these

---

1. The opinion that in the earliest periods of time mankind in every
part of the globe were in a state of absolute savagism, forms the basis
of Lord Kaimes' well known work called *Sketches of the History of Man*.
The late Dr. Doeg of Sterling, replied to Lord Kaimes, in *Two Letters
on the Savage State*. Illustrating all his positions by a great number of
particulars from ancient and modern history, among other proposi-
tions, Dr. Doeg established the following:

> The more populous kingdoms were civilized at a period prior to
> the records of history, and the presumption therefore is, that they
> were civilized from the beginning.
> No people once civilized, and then again reduced to barbarism,
> have ever recovered without foreign aid.
> No savage nation has ever been known to move one step to-
> wards civilization, till impelled by some external cause.
> There appears in savages a natural and rooted aversion to a
> civilized state.
> There seems to be in human nature an innate propensity towards
> degeneracy, even in a state of the highest improvement.

And in concluding, he challenged Lord Kaimes to point to one
state, nation, or society, once confessedly savage, which ever did,
solely by the gradual exertion of its own internal powers, after passing successively through the steps and states specified in Lord
Kaimes' sketches, at length arrive at civilization.

Shortly after the publication of these *Letters*, Lord Kaimes invited
the doctor to visit him, when, after much discussion, his Lordship
candidly and fully acknowledged himself in error and his opponent
right.

Dr. Doeg traced the "idea of a state of universal savagism to the
chimerical cosmogonies of Mochus, Democritus and Epicurus." We

rights and all those various subordinations of personal condition, which are necessary to the perfection of society and to the full development of humanity, are strictly and perfectly natural. That is as truly natural to which nature in its progress invariably conducts us, as that which is actually been with us.

The acquired perceptions of sight are no less natural than those which are original.

If, therefore, the "state of nature," commonly so called, be a mere dream of the imagination, what are we to say of "natural rights," as founded upon that fictitious basement?

We say that, as to an absolute equality among men, it neither has existed nor does exist as a fact; nor yet is it any where demanded by the Scriptures.

The Poet well says:

> Tell the truth, yea, tell it out,
> *Nature!* without tear or doubt —
> Tell it out that never yet
> Have two utter equals met.
> Leaves and fruits on every tree,
> Fowls and fish of air and sea,
> Stars on high with all their host,
> Pebbles from a Kingdom's coast,
> Search them all, some difference still
> Clings to each, for good or ill;

---

see only one difference between this idea and that of the author of the *Vestiges*, — one goes a little further back than the other. Lord Kaimes develops civilized man out of a *savage*, — the other writer out of an *oyster!* But Christian minds that shrink with horror from the one theory are quite familiar with the other, all contrary as it is to Bible history.

Search the world – all worlds around,
Perfect twins were never found;
Babes of various realm and race,
Men of every age and place;
Gifts of God, or wise denials,
Pleasures, sorrows, triumphs, trials:
All things differ every where, –
Never two could start quite fair –
Never two could keep the start,
In soul or body, mind or heart;
While the shortest winter's day.
To its morrow gloom'd away.

And, *as to the Bible,* it gives no countenance to the common radical notions on this subject. It teaches, indeed, that we are *all brethren.* But Esau and Jacob were brethren of whom, before the children were born or had yet done good or evil, God said, "The elder shall serve the younger." The Bible presents God as the sovereign Arbiter of human affairs, dividing to the nations their inheritance – yes, and "setting every individual member in the (great social) body just as it hath pleased him" (1 Cor. 12:18). The subjection, by God, of one man and one nation to another man and another nation, is supposed throughout the Bible as an ordinary and constantly recurring fact. The Christian fathers, too, for many centuries after Christ, are totally silent as to any opposition of Christianity to slavery. It was a common saying among them, however, that slavery is not man's natural state, but a result of the fall – in other words, they viewed it as one of the allotments of Providence to man, as having sinned and so forfeited liberty and every other blessing with life itself.

In this day of wide spread agitation about rights of liberty, and of rising agitation too about rights of property rent, land, &c, the Bible is our stronghold. In the Tenth Commandment, graven with God's finger on marble, we find a divine solemn recognition of *rights of property*: "Thou shalt not covet anything that is thy neighbors'." Do you find yourself *without things,* that is, *poor?* See that you do not even wish in your heart to have your neighbor's things, however abundantly the sovereign but righteous Lord of all may have bestowed them upon him in contrast with yourself. The same divine Commandment sanctions even the *right of property in a human being,* and thus gives warrant to our rights of authority as slave holders. The Lawgiver says, "Thou shalt not covet thy neighbor's manservant, nor his maidservant, nor his ox, nor his ass, nor any thing that is thy neighbor's." Does the almighty God then count slaves as human cattle? Is the slave a mere thing? Far from it! He is an immortal man, but has a human master by God's appointment, and that master has a right of property in him – has a right in his services which no other man can innocently covet. Nay, the slave himself must not covet or take what belongs not to himself. But on the contrary, it is said to him, "Art thou called being a slave, care not for it" (1 Cor. 7:21).[2]

---

2. On the other clause we quote, without any expression of opinion, a note from Babington's Hulsean Lecture on the *Influence of Christianity in Promoting the Abolition of Slavery in Europe,* p. 15:

> The doubt is what *if* (not expressed in the Greek) means; several very eminent commentators quoted in Pool's *Synopsis,* and also Usher and Neander say, "liberty:" but Chrysostom, Jerome, Theodoret, Isidorus, Pelusiota, Œcumenius, Photius, and Theophylact explain "it" by "slavery"; and this sense, it must be confessed, suits the context

The Scriptures then did not originate the idea that all men, simply from the fact of being *men*, have a natural right to an equal amount of property, or an equal share of personal liberty. There are rights unquestionably, which belong to man as such, and which can not be wrested from him without the destruction of his intellectual and moral constitution. Without them he could not be a *man*. But there are other rights which accrue in the progress of society, and which appertain not to man *as such*, but to man in particular providential circumstances and relations. These rights are as natural as others, because society and civilization, which develop them, are natural; but they cannot be separated from the circumstances and relations which determine them; and hence, men in other circumstances and other relations can lay no claim to them.

It is a mistake to suppose that because these rights are *natural*, therefore they belong to humanity, essentially considered, and must accordingly be conceded to every human being, because he is a man. The rights of a father are natural, but they belong only to fathers. Rights of property are natural, but they belong only to those who have property. There is a natural way of becoming a father, and there is a natural method of acquiring and indefinitely increasing property.

Where then do we place the foundation of all rights? In the nature which God has given to man. It is that which ren-

---

admirably; not to add that ει και commonly signifies not "if" but "although." See Cramer's *Catena in Epist. Paul.* 5: I, p. 141, for some of these authorities. Chrysostom mentions that others took the verse quite the opposite way, and Saverianus, his contemporary, appears to have done so. Cramer, 1. c.

ders him capable of rights. A brute can neither have property nor dominion; for rights can no where exist, except among those who are susceptible of moral obligation.

Of course, therefore, all those rights which belong to men as such, should be conceded to the race. None should any where be deprived of them. But the rights which belong to particular conditions – those which result from the circumstances and relations in which men are placed – must obviously admit of as great a variety as those circumstances and relations themselves; and these rights are distributed under the providence of God, according to those laws (as natural as society itself,) in conformity with which men come to be found in these circumstances and relations. Some are rulers, some subjects; some are rich, some poor; some are fathers, some children; some are bond, some free. And if a man is justly and providentially a ruler, he has the rights of a ruler; if a husband, the rights of a husband; if a father, the rights of a father; and if a slave, only the rights of a slave. Hence the force and propriety of the legal maxim: *Partus sequitur ventrem* – that is, all men have an equal and perfect right to the status in which they are born, with all its established rights and privileges, and also to whatever else they can legally and meritoriously acquire. Our true and only titles to liberty and property are *inheritance,* or *honest and legal acquisition,* (both dependent upon the discriminations of Providence,) and not any *abstract natural equality,* stepping in at every succeeding age, among the social and political inequalities necessarily produced even in one generation, and laying all level in confusion and destruction. We hold such an equality to be –

> A dull, debasing, sordid thing,
> Crushing down each generous spring;
> A stern Procrustes' iron bed,
> To rack the feet or lop the head.

It is nothing but –

> Vanity and Sloth and Crime that stand,
> With low Ambition hand to hand.
> And scheme and plot a cunning plan,
> Utterly to ruin man;
> They seek to level love and hate,
> And grind to atoms all things great.

The only way of evading the statements now made, as far as slavery is concerned, is to deny that this condition is consistent with the appointments of Providence, or the will of God – in other words, to assert (as we both wonder and regret to see the Prudential Committee of the American Board asserting) that slavery is "Anti-Christian and always and every where sinful." That cannot be Anti-Christian however, which Christ and the Apostles never condemned. And slavery must just be left to stand upon the same footing with any other inequality of condition, until some higher revelation than the Bible's shall shew that the revelation itself is inconsistent with the moral nature of man, and deprives him of his ethick character; – in other words, that man cannot be a slave, and yet fear God and work righteousness.

That these were the principles of the English and American Revolutions, is obvious from the fact that the patriotic actors in those great events professed to contend for nothing but a lawful inheritance; – rights which had long before been connected with the circumstances and relations in which they were providentially placed. "Your subjects have *inherited* this freedom,"[3] was the language of the *petition of right* (drawn by Selden and other profoundly

---

3. Macauley, in his recently published *History* remarks, Vol. 1, p. 23:

> The change, great as it is, which the policy of England has undergone during the last six centuries, has been the effect of gradual development, not of demolition and reconstruction. The present Constitution of our country is, to the Constitution under which she flourished five hundred years ago, what the tree is to the sapling, what the man is to the boy. The alteration has been great. Yet there never was a moment, at which, the chief part of what existed was not old....
>
> Other Societies possess written constitutions more symmetrical; but no other society has yet succeeded in uniting revolution with prescription, progress with stability, the energy of youth with the majesty of immemorial antiquity....
>
> There is no country where statesmen have been so much under the influence of the past....
>
> History is (by us) regarded as a repository of title-deeds, on which the rights of governments and nations depend....
>
> Our laws and customs have never been lost in general and irreparable ruin. With us, the precedents of the middle ages are still valid precedents, and are still cited on the gravest occasions by the most eminent statesmen. Thus, when King George III. was attacked by the malady which made him incapable of performing his regal functions, and when the most distinguished lawyers and politicians differed widely as to the course which ought to be pursued, the houses of Parliament would not proceed to discuss any plan of regency, till all the examples which were to be found in our annals, from the earliest times, had been collected and arranged. Committees were appointed to examine the ancient records of the realm. The first precedent reported was that of the year 1217: much importance was attached to the precedents of 1326, of 1377, and of 1422; but the case which was justly considered as most in point was that of 1455. Thus, in our country, the dearest interests of parties have frequently been staked on the results of the researches of antiquaries.

learned men,) and addressed by Parliament to Charles I. To that Parliament which resisted Charles' encroachments on their inherited rights are due the thanks of their American as much as of their English posterity. We repudiate the popular idea that our Revolution freed us from British slavery. We were no slaves. Our fathers contended for their lawful franchises, not on abstract principles as the *rights of men,* but on legal principles as the *rights of Englishmen,* and as a patrimony derived from their forefathers.

But we are only laying down general principles. We do not forget that every case of revolution is to be decided on its own merits. "Times and occasions teach their own lessons." "Circumstances (which with some pass for nothing,) give in reality to every political principle its distinguishing color and its discriminating effect." We have undertaken to set forth the general bearing of Christianity on human rights. We understand the general doctrine of the Scriptures to be, that a nation, and that individuals, who enjoy political freedom, have the same, and no other, right to it which the rich man's son has to the property he was born to; and that other nations or individuals, born under despotic governments, are bound to submit to the inequalities of their position, just as the poor man's child who inherits nothing; unless like many a poor man's son he can legally and meritoriously acquire what he has not inherited. If a monarch is born to the arbitrary sway of millions, or a slaveholder to the rule of hundreds, the Bible teaches respecting both, that Cæsar has his "things" which must be rendered to him. If the subjects of either Cæsar refuse him his "things" they sin. If they seek to wrest away his rights that they may increase their own, they commit the same fault, as if the many poor should rise and forcibly take away the possessions of the few rich. Nations and individuals have no scriptural right to get either freedom or property in this way. They are in God's hands, who has put upon them this burden, and they must be content to remain in God's hands, doing their duty in the place He has appointed them.

Do we then maintain the doctrine of *passive obedience?* We regret this error of the "old exploded fanatics" of slavery with as much abhorrence as we do that of our "new fanatics," of equal universal freedom.[4] Magistrates and kings, and masters too, are to be obeyed as such, and not otherwise. The veriest despot on earth is obeyed as one that has arbitrary, yet not unlimited power. If the Shah of Persia were to prove himself a human tiger, immolating his subjects, just to please his infernal cruelty, we say that, even under that despotism, Christianity would authorize the nation, not *any individual,* but *the nation collectively,* to

---

4. According to Edmund Burke:

> The speculative line of demarcation where obedience ought to end and resistance must begin is indeed faint, obscure, and not easily definable. It is not a single act or a single event which determines it. Governments must be abused and deranged indeed, before it can be thought of, and the prospect of the future must be as bad as the experience of the past. When things are in that lamentable condition, the nature of the disease is to indicate the remedy, to those whom nature has qualified to administer in extremities this critical, ambiguous, bitter potion to a distempered state.... [A] revolution will always be the very last resource of the thinking and the good (*Maxim, Opinions, and Characters,* page 78).

But even here the general principle is very plain.

put him off his throne.[5] "Tyranny from policy may justify rebellion from principle." God made the Shah of Persia a despot, but He gave him no authority to kill after that fashion. That is not one of "Cæsar's things."

So, much more under a constitutional government, the people have a right, nay, are bound to defend what Providence has given them, – what they have *inherited,* whether of liberty or of property. The Commons of England had a right to resist the encroachments of Charles I. The English nation, in 1688, had a right to resist the second James. And our fathers of the Revolution had a right to contend for their old inheritance, as Britons, of the right of being represented where they were to be taxed.

Thus, according to our views of the Christian doctrine on this subject, the duties and the rights of nations both differ according to their circumstances. Of some, the duty is obedience and submission to authority even the most arbitrary; while others may have to guard watchfully, and faithfully defend their inheritance of freedom. Their duties differ, because their providential position differs. They may

---

5. In this connexion it is well worth our while to observe the method by which God delivered His chosen people from the land of Egypt. Though in bondage to Idolaters, who oppressed them in the most cruel manner, they strike not one blow for themselves, nor take one step in flight, till the authority which God had put them under was made willing to say, "Get ye out." So too, at a later day, when captives in Babylon, they were directed, "seek the peace of the city, whither I have caused you to be carried captives, and pray unto the Lord for it, for in the peace thereof ye shall have peace." Jer. xxix: 7. Waiting through the whole period of 70 years, they were peacefully led back to their own land, as God disposed the heart of Cyrus to favour their return.

be servants of their despot, and then they must obey. They may be masters of their public servants, and then they must see that these do faithfully perform their various offices and functions.

We would not deny that there has been in the affairs of men, under providential guidance, a progress of liberty. And this progress of liberty it may be the will of the Almighty Ruler to extend, until free institutions become universal. Nor yet do we deny that, in the providence of God, liberty has often changed hands. Nor would we question that the most wicked and bloody revolutions may be by God over-ruled, for the final general good. We believe all events are so over-ruled. Still, such a merciful divine interposition does not exculpate the guilty movers of rebellion.[6] We hold to the general principle before stated, that every soul must be subject to the higher powers, for there is no power but of God.

It may be said that we have written to no purpose, seeing that we have only set forth very general principles. But we think the principles we have set forth are neither more nor less general than the Bible's. We have developed, as we think, the scriptural doctrine of human rights. The world is governed by ideas. "Theories industrial, social and political – abstract opinions, Utopian dreams are upheaving the old world." The new is also agitated by a theory – the theory of free soil and free slaves – yes, and "questions in obscurer channels, about rent and property, and the right to labor, and to the land, are spreading themselves

6. See all these sentiments fully sustained in Calvin's *Institutes*, Book IV, Chapter xx, Sections xxix, xxx and xxxi.

through the land." Thousands are proclaiming that there is
no right of property in human beings, and *hundreds have
begun to shout* that there is no right of rent, and that no man
has a right to any more land than he can cultivate. Against
all these general principles we set ours, – nay, not *ours*, but
those of God's inspired Word.

It is indeed a very practical, and not at all a mere abstract question; what is the influence of Christianity upon
slavery – upon the *slave*, upon the *master*, and upon the
permanency of the relation?

It has been said by a Northern divine that, "if the gospel were as evangelically preached at the South as it is at
the North," (say in New England,) "slavery would soon
come to an end." The Prudential Committee of the American Board, also, in their letter to the Choctaw Missionaries,
say, that if our Saviour's golden rule "were carried out to
its legitimate results, slavery in all its essential features
would cease at once."

But what is slavery? There is no end to this discussion,
because different parties use *slavery* to mean very different
things. Dr. Whewell's definition prevails, we suppose, very
generally in New England. "Slavery converts a person into
a thing, an object merely passive, without any of the recognized attributes of human nature."

This was Aristotle's idea when he advised Alexander
to deal with the Barbarians as with brutes or plants. This
was the spirit, and letter too, of the Roman law, which held
slaves, *"pro nullis, pro mortuis, pro quadrupedibus."* But these
are not our modern, our Southern ideas of slavery. And old
school Presbyterians at the North have given another, and
what we take as the true definition of the term, "All the

ideas (says the *Biblical Repertory*) which necessarily enter into the definition of slavery are, deprivation of personal liberty, obligation of service at the discretion of another, and the transferable character of the authority and claim of the master." It may be that some bad, very bad laws have been passed to regulate slavery. There may be some unchristian abuses of the master's power – some sinful accessories attaching to the institution – but the essence of slavery is the master's right to use and control and dispose of the services of his slave.

Now Christianity *unquestionably sanctions slavery,* as thus defined. This is one manifest bearing of Christianity upon the institution. We do not say that Christianity sanctions slavery as Aristotle sanctioned it, when he said that the Greeks might rightfully go and by war reduce the Barbarians into bondage. But we think we are often so misunderstood at the North. Our statement that the Bible sanctions slavery arouses much needless indignation, because the North will not distinguish between the right to govern our Slaves, as being providentially placed under our control, and the right of going and enslaving men free-born.

And here we will refer to another expression of opinion at the South, which very likely is often misunderstood. Southern politicians say, "Slavery is a positive blessing." In the fear of God we, and all other Christians that we know of, say the same thing, *absolutely,* as respects the Negro. As respects the whole community of Whites and Blacks, whom an unscrutable but wise Providence has joined here together, we also say the same thing, *as comparing slavery with emancipation.* But as comparing the present advantages of our White population with what they might have been, had not the Negro been introduced, the Christian people of the South have never yet said that slavery is a positive blessing, and we know not that they will ever be driven by all the fierceness of the attacks upon them to say so. Why should they say so, or why should they say the contrary? Why waste time in vain speculations about unsupposable cases, when we have so much practical duty not yet over-taken?

We repeat, Christianity sanctions the relation of master and slave. The Bible is the best book for those who are low down as well as for those who are high up in the scale of life. It suits people living under a despotic government, quite as well as it suits those who live under a free govern-ment. It is as safe a book for the subjects of the one as for the sons of the other.

But Christianity also civilizes the slave. It is as good for slaves, however fierce and ungovernable naturally, as it is for the convicts of the penitentiary, or the lunatics of the asylum. Not that it renders force always unnecessary. We must keep a rod for the backs of wayward children and slaves, if not for those of soldiers and seamen. But men are no where on earth governed mainly by force. Moral means are mightiest, and of all moral means Christianity is the purest and the strongest. The British government once dreaded, but now fosters, the influence of the missionaries, even the American missionaries, in India.

In a word, Christianity improves the slave in all parts of his character. It takes away piece-meal the mass of bar-barian ignorance, superstition and corruption. It is advan-tageous to their whole physical, intellectual and moral na-ture. It makes the slaves better, more intelligent, industrious, tractable, trusty, – better men, better servants of God, better servants of man. "The slave," says Neander, in reference to the first three centuries, (Vol. 1, p. 71, Rose's translation,) "remained in all his worldly circumstances a slave, and fulfilled his duties in that station with greater fidelity and conscientiousness than before." The same is true of our Negroes. Christianity has improved them, both as men and as slaves. Compare them with their forefathers! By how many degrees the barbarian has already been elevated in all parts of his nature.

And what is the effect of Christianity upon the master?

It softens his spirit, in the sternness of law and discipline, while it confirms and establishes their just bonds. Whatever was formerly harsh in the relation is gradually removed. Mutual intercourse is sweetened by it – the master is no tyrant, the slave no rebel. "Authority ceases to be severe; obedience ceases to be a task." The essence of slavery, viz, the master's right to use and dispose of his servant's time and labor, is untouched by Christianity, except to establish it on a moral and religious foundation, and yet the master learns to feel that he and his slave are children of the same God and Father, and while he cannot admit him to the social privileges of a brother, he recognizes in him a valued and esteemed, though humble, dependent. And this effect of Christianity on the master grows with the growth and advance of the legitimate influence of Christianity on the slave. Good slaves make good masters, as well as good masters good slaves.

And then there is an influence of Christianity in removing the abuses which may attach to the exercise of arbitrary power.

It was so under the Roman empire. Under Augustus, Adrian and Antoninus, putting slaves to death was no murder, but the first Christian emperor laid down that "if any one, after the brutal manner of the barbarians, caused his slave to expire under the torture, he should be guilty of homicide."

So also he made a law (A.D. 398) forbidding the forcible separation of servile families, whether by sale or partition of property. "For who can endure (said he) that children and parents, wives and husbands, should be separated from each other?"

Clement of Alexandria, who lived in the 3rd century, says, "We must do by our slaves as we would do by ourselves, for they are men as we are; for God, if you consider, is the God of the freeman and of the slave alike."

And so Christianity makes us feel now. We recognize our slaves as not being things, but men. When we buy and sell them, it is not *human flesh and blood* we buy and sell, but we buy or sell a *right*, established by Providence, and sanctioned by Scripture, to their *labor and service for life*. We still bear in mind that they are men, and have immortal souls; – that Christ shed His blood to redeem them as well as ourselves, and that we are put in charge of their training, as of that of our own children, for His Kingdom and glory.

It is, then, as plain as daylight, that Christianity condemns all laws of the State, and all ideas and practices of individuals, which put aside the immortality of the slave and regard him in any other light than that of a moral and responsible fellow-creature of our own. We have no hesitation in declaring that we accord with Judge O'Neall in earnestly desiring the repeal, for example, of the law against teaching the slave to read. Not that we suppose it possible for the laboring class in any country to make much actual use of reading – nor that we forget how the Apostles converted a world by oral teaching chiefly; but because we conceive the law referred to is both useless and hurtful. *It is a useless law,* for very many of our best citizens continually break it, or allow it to be broken in their families. Besides, very many of our slaves can read, and do teach and will teach others. No dangerous Negro can be hindered from getting knowledge by such a law. "It sharpens our appetite," said an old Negro in Savannah to an English traveller and writer. But the law is *hurtful,* inasmuch as it throws an obstacle in the way of that which it is plainly the wisdom of the State to foster and encourage, viz., the religious instruction of the young Negro population.

The question of the effect of Christianity upon the permanency of slavery in this country, is one certainly of the profoundest interest. What light does the past history of Christianity shed upon it?

Adam Smith, Hallam, and Macauley also, in his recent *History of England,* all speak of the abolition of slavery in Europe as having been very silently and imperceptibly effected, neither by legislative regulation nor physical force. What share Christianity had in effecting this abolition, has been much disputed. Guizot, Muratori, Millar, Sismondi, and the Pictorial Historian of England, allow her very little influence. On the other hand, Robinson, the historian of Charles V, Biot, an elaborate French author, who got a gold medal from the French Academy of Moral and Political Science, for his work *De l'Abolition de l'esclavage ancien en occident,* and the Rev. Churchill Babington, of St. John's College, Cambridge, who got the Hulsean prize for the year 1845, for an essay on the same subject, all these, and others, ascribe the greatest influence to Christianity, as the only influence which has lasted long enough, or been universal enough, or unmixed and constant enough to accomplish such a task.

But it is curious indeed, as a question of historical philosophy, to see how exceedingly *gradual* was the process by which Christianity operated in the abolition of slavery.

Not only Guizot, on the one side, declares (Guiz. *Civilis. en Europe*, Sec. vi., p. 14,) that, "Slavery subsisted a long time in the bosom of Christian society, without any great horror or irritation being expressed against it," but Biot, on the other side, tells us that "no Christian writers of the first three centuries speak of the abolition of slavery as a consequence of Christianity." – Biot, p. 26. And Babington, after quoting many passages from Basil, Chrysostom, Jerome, and other early fathers remarks, "Not one of these writers even hints that slavery is improper or unlawful." Page 29.

This same writer also refers to the fact that Christianity has for eighteen centuries been operating upon European servitude. Page 117. He also remarks, "Christianity has been constantly producing such an effect upon society that when a thousand years had passed away, strict personal slavery had, in most parts of Europe, begun to disappear." Page 180.

What then is that influence, which, in our day, is so clamorous for the abolition of slavery? It is, certainly, not Christianity; for Christianity, both in the days of the Apostles, and for centuries afterwards, did never so lift her voice. Christianity operated and operates in a much pro-founder, far gentler, and more wholesome manner.

What then is it? It is partly *humanity* excited by exaggerated, and in a great degree, false statements – it is partly *political self-interest and jugglery* – and it is partly the *democratic* principle. It is the radical doctrine of "equal rights," – it is the idea that the slave is unjustly deprived of or debarred from his natural rights – that he is entitled to liberty and prepared for it.

Let Christians at the North take their stand, if they will, but let them do it distinctly and fairly, and openly, as apostles of civil liberty, – and let them preach a crusade for natural rights. But, let them not tell us that their Master came to do such a work, or that the Gospel, evangelically preached, would soon put an end to slavery. Let not Mr. Treat, or any one else, tell us that the law of love, if applied between slave holders and their slaves, would immediately rupture the bonds of society amongst us. Unchristian abuses that law has reformed and is reforming, and (when the public mind at the South shall be no longer stung to madness by insults and reproaches,) will still reform. But the essence of slavery – the master's right to his slave's labor – is no more assaulted by Christianity than are the property rights of rich men at the North. The true interpretation of the golden rule on the subject of slavery is to be found in the Apostolic instructions to masters. If there be any better way of applying the law of love to the system of slavery than these rules set forth, why did not the Apostles who said so much to masters shew it to us, instead of leaving it to be found out by the men of this age?

Are we then asked whether we believe slavery among

us will be perpetual? We say, as far as Christianity is concerned, we do not see why it might not be perpetual, and
yet we do not see reason to say that it will be so. It is a
question for speculation, or rather it is not a question for
speculation, for how can we judge beforehand what God
intends to do? It is then more properly a question of Providence. It is in God's hands, and there we wish it to be.

We cannot reason that Christianity will operate now as
it did of old upon slavery, because new elements have
come in. There is the new element of democracy on the one
hand, which may not allow Christianity to work in its own
healthful and peaceful way – which sneers at such declara-
tions as Bishop Butler made when he said, "Men are impa-
tient and for precipitating things, but the Author of nature,
(and the Bible,) appears deliberate throughout His operations," – and which would serve the most complicated
questions and the most tangled relations, as Alexander did
the Gordian Knot.

On the other hand, there is the new element of a *difference of race*. Of old there was no similar obstacle to emancipation. Will Christianity ever allow us to manumit here our
three millions of Africans – our three millions increased to
five or ten millions? Will Christianity, that unquestionably
makes masters benevolent, ever satisfy us that it is possible
for two such dissimilar races to dwell together on equal
terms?

Or will Christianity and the Providence of God ever
point out a way for their removal to their own or some
other country? We count it almost profane to hazard one
speculation about such hidden things of God.

One thing, fellow citizens of the South, is plain! It is

ours to do the duties of intelligent, decided, fearless, conscientious Christian masters, and future events we may leave with Him, who will direct them well.

And let our Northern Christian brethren join us in leaving Divine Providence to work out His own plans. We say to them respectfully and kindly, cease your attempts to rouse our consciences about the sinfulness of slavery. Dismiss your anxieties about the civil liberty of the slave. He does not need that – it would be no blessing to him. He needs another and a better freedom. That is the great point. Exhort us, reprove us, rebuke us, help us, pray for us in reference to this point! You have begun at the wrong end. You would abolish that which must be, and ought to be, fortified and confirmed. The master's authority must not be withdrawn. Our system of slavery is a civilizer and a Christianizer. We must leave it for God to remove, when His time comes; meanwhile, we must maintain it, always administering it according to the law of love as explained by the Apostles.

The American Board has long stood fast and firm on the high scriptural ground respecting slavery. At their meeting in Brooklyn, some years ago, all the tremendous pressure that was brought by Abolitionists to bear upon them could not drive them from maintaining that slaveholding cannot scripturally be made a test of church communion. And it would indeed seem hard, that they who have nothing directly to do with slavery in these States, should, because unwilling to take the position of a lever to act on us, be made to share with us the burden of popular odium at the North. But, very remarkably indeed, the Providence of God has actually thrown upon that body an immediate responsibility in this matter. In two of their missions among the Indians of this country, slavery exists. Their church members hold slaves; their missionaries hire them, which is, in principle of course, the same as owning them. The Abolitionists are now urging a new issue on the Board. If slave-holding Indians can not be excluded from missionary churches, at least the missionary must be prohibited from hiring slave labor, however necessary to the comfort of his family, and however impossible it may be to obtain any other kind of domestic assistance. We shall await with interest the next meeting of the Board, to see how they will dispose of this question.

But the Prudential Committee, in their correspondence through their Secretary, Mr. Treat, with the Cherokee and Choctaw missions, have already submitted to the missions the alternative of giving up either slave labor, or their schools. We would make one single observation on this point. If those Indian missionaries are morally bound thus to abjure slavery as "a system always and every where sinful," why are not all we, who live in the American Slave States, morally bound to do the same thing? But, does the Prudential Committee mean to declare that, in their judgment, all Christian ministers and Christian people at the South should at once relinquish slave labor as sinful? In other words, (since the example of all the Christian people would be of course omnipotent,) would they wish to see the South plunged into all the horrors of emancipation?

The Committee are much changed from what they were, if they would take this ground. But if the system must necessarily be maintained, then who has any right to blame good men for aiding to maintain it?

But the Committee do, in Mr. Treat's letter, cast censure upon all such good men. That letter holds their slaveholding to be *"prima facie* evidence of guilt." Here is a man, (says Mr. Treat,) involved in a system unchristian and sinful, and yet, (dreadful presumption indeed,) "he requests admission to the table of our blessed Lord." Yes! and Mr. Treat does not hesitate to say, that the Christian missionary or minister must stop the slaveholder as he approaches the communion table, and require him to "prove," (what the Apostles have left no trace of their requiring the slaveholding candidate in their day to prove,) viz: "his freedom from the guilt of the system, before he can make good his claim to a place among the followers of Christ." "Such an enquiry, (says Mr. Treat,) is in all cases fundamental." We only reply, shew us your proofs.

As to the paragraph which follows this statement of the principles, upon which alone any slaveholder can, according to this letter, be, in any case, admitted to church fellowship, we have only to say in concluding this article, that *it cuts off all the Southern churches*. Not one benevolent Christian master in a thousand at the South could shew that he is "an involuntary slaveholder;" that he "retains the relation at the request of his slaves, and for their advantage;" or that he "utterly rejects and repudiates the idea of holding property in his fellow-men." And if the American Board should take the ground of Mr. Treat, that there is "no warrant whatever for receiving any but such slaveholders to the privileges of the people of God," then we cannot see but they will have yielded every thing to the Abolitionists, and that we must be cut off, (as we shall then be well content to be cut off,) from their fellowship.

A native of Charleston, South Carolina, John B. Adger (1810-1899) was educated at Union College, New York and Princeton Theological Seminary, New Jersey. He was ordained to the ministry in 1834, and he and his wife served as missionaries to the Armenians in Smyrna for twelve years. Forced by poor health to retire from the field in 1847, he returned to Charleston and took up the work of preaching to the Negroes of the city in the basement of Second Presbyterian Church. The following year, he was instrumental in the erection of a new building, devoted exclusively to the slave population, and he served as pastor of that congregation for five years (1847-1852). Adger later worked as a teacher at the Presbyterian Theological Seminary at Columbia, South Carolina.

The preceding article appeared in the *Southern Presbyterian Review*, March 1849, Vol. II, No. 4.

II

Report on Slavery
by Rev. James Henley Thornwell, D.D. LL.D.

It will be remembered that at the Sessions of this Synod in Columbia, in 1847, a series of resolutions was presented, setting forth the relations of the Church to slavery, and the duties respectively of masters and servants. After some discussion, it was deemed advisable to appoint a committee to take the whole subject into consideration, and submit a report, somewhat in the form of a circular letter to all the Churches of Jesus Christ throughout the earth, explaining the position of Southern Christians, and vindicating their right to the confidence, love and fellowship of all who every where call upon the name of our common Master. The design of appointing this committee was not to increase, but to allay agitation. It was evident that a strong public sentiment, both in Europe and America, had been organized, and was daily growing in intensity, against institutions which we had inherited from our fathers, and against which we felt no call, either from religion or policy, to enter a protest.

We felt it to be due to Christian charity to make an effort, however unsuccessfully, to disabuse the minds of brethren, with whom we were anxious to maintain the unity of the spirit in the bonds of peace, of prejudices and misapprehensions which we were confident had misled them. Events have taken place since the appointment of the committee, which invest the subject with additional importance. At that time the greatest danger immediately apprehended was a partial alienation, perhaps an external schism, among those who were as one in a common faith. But now, more portentous calamities are dreaded. The determined zeal with which a policy founded, for the most part, in the conviction that slavery is a sin, is pressed upon the Federal Legislature, justifies the gloomiest forebodings in relation to the integrity of the Union and the stability of our free institutions. The question has passed from the Church to the State; it is no longer a debate among Christian ministers and Christian men, as to the terms of communion and the rights of particular communities to the Christian name. It is now a question as to the equality of the States which compose this great commonwealth of nations, and the obligation of the charter which binds them in federal alliance. The immense importance which, in this aspect, is given to the subject, has induced the Chairman of your Committee to present, upon his own responsibility, the following thoughts. He has been unable to consult the brethren who were appointed with him. And as he is deeply convinced that the position of the Southern, and perhaps, he may say, of the whole Presbyterian Church, in relation to slavery, is the only position which can save the country from disaster and the Church from schism, he is quickened by the double consideration of patriotism and religion to record opinions which, however hastily expressed, have been maturely weighed.

I. The relation of the Church to slavery cannot be definitely settled without an adequate apprehension of the nature and office of the Church itself. What, then, is the Church? It is not, as we fear too many are disposed to regard it, a moral institute of universal good, whose business it is to wage war upon every form of human ill, whether social, civil, political or moral, and to patronize every expedient which a romantic benevolence may suggest as likely to contribute to human comfort, or to mitigate the inconveniences of life. We freely grant, and sincerely rejoice in the truth, that the healthful operations of the Church, in its own appropriate sphere, react upon all the interests of man, and contribute to the progress and prosperity of society; but we are far from admitting either that it is the purpose of God, that, under the present dispensation of religion, all ill shall be banished from this sublunary state, and earth be converted into a paradise, or that the proper end of the Church is the direct promotion of universal good. It has no commission to construct society afresh, to adjust its elements in different proportions, to re-arrange the distribution of its classes, or to change the forms of its political constitutions. The noble schemes of philanthropy which have distinguished Christian nations; their magnificent foundations for the poor, the maimed and the blind; the efforts of the wise and good to mitigate human misery, and to temper justice with mercy in the penal visitations of the law; the various associations that have been formed to check and abate particular forms of evil, have all been quickened into life by the spirit of Christianity. But still it

is not the distinctive province of the Church to build asy-
lums for the needy or insane; to organize societies for the
improvement of the penal code, or for arresting the progress of intemperance, gambling or lust. The problems
which the anomalies of our fallen state are continually
forcing on philanthropy, the Church has no right directly
to solve. She must leave them to the Providence of God
and to human wisdom, sanctified and guided by the spiritual influences which it is her glory to foster and cherish.

The Church is a very peculiar society – voluntary in the
sense that all its members become so, not by constraint, but
willingly; but not in the sense that its doctrines, discipline
and order, are the creatures of human will, deriving their
authority and obligation from the consent of its members.
On the contrary, it has a fixed and unalterable constitution;
and that constitution is the Word of God. It is the Kingdom
of the Lord Jesus Christ. He is enthroned in it as a sovereign. It can hear no voice but His; obey no commands but
His; pursue no ends but His. Its officers are His servants,
bound to execute only His will. Its doctrines are His teachings, which He, as a prophet, has given from God; its discipline His law, which He as king has ordained. The power
of the Church, accordingly, is only ministerial and declara-
tive. The Bible, and the Bible alone, is her rule of faith and
practice. She can announce what it teaches; enjoin what it
commands; prohibit what it condemns, and enforce her
testimonies by spiritual sanctions. Beyond the Bible she can
never go, and apart from the Bible she can never speak. To
the law and to the testimony, and to them alone, she must
always appeal; and when they are silent it is her duty to
put her hand upon her lips. These principles, thus abstract-

ly stated, are not likely to provoke opposition, but the conclusion which flows from them, and for the sake of which
we have here stated them, has unfortunately been too much
disregarded; and that is, that the Church is not at liberty to
speculate. She has a *creed*, but no *opinions*. When she speaks,
it must be in the name of the Lord, and her only argument
is, *thus it is written*.

In conformity with this principle, has the Church any
authority to declare slavery to be sinful? Or, in other
words, has the Bible, anywhere, either directly or indirectly, condemned the relation of master and servant as
incompatible with the will of God?

We think there can be little doubt, that if the Church
had universally repressed the spirit of speculation, and had
been content to stand by the naked testimony of God, we
should have been spared many of the most effective disser-
tations against slavery. Deduct the opposition to it which
has arisen from sympathy with imaginary sufferings, from
ignorance of its nature and misapplication of the crotchets
of philosophers – deduct the opposition which is due to
sentiment, romance or speculation, and how much will be
found to have originated from the humble and devout
study of the Scriptures? Will any man say that he who applies to them with an honest and unprejudiced mind, and
discusses their teachings upon the subject, simply as a
question of language and interpretation, will rise from the
pages with the sentiments or spirit of a modern Abolitionist? Certain it is that no direct condemnation of it can anywhere be found in the sacred volume. A social element in
all states, from the dawn of history until the present period, if it be the crying and damning sin which its enemies

represent it to be, it is truly amazing that the Bible, which professes to be a lamp to our feet and a light to our path, to make the man of God perfect, thoroughly furnished unto every good work, no where gives the slightest caution against this tremendous evil. The master is no where rebuked as a monster of cruelty and tyranny – the slave no where exhibited as the object of peculiar compassion and sympathy. The manner in which the relation itself is spoken of and its duties prescribed, the whole tone and air of the sacred writers convey the impression that they themselves had not the least suspicion that they were dealing with a subject full of abominations and outrages. We read their language – cool, dispassioned, didactic. We find masters exhorted in the same connection with husbands, parents, magistrates; slaves exhorted in the same connection with wives, children and subjects. The Prophet or Apostle gives no note of alarm – raises no signal of distress when he comes to the slave and his master, and the unwary reader is in serious danger of concluding that according to the Bible, it is not much more harm to be a master than a father – a slave than a child. But this is not all.

The Scriptures not only fail to condemn – they as distinctly sanction slavery as any other social condition of man. The Church was organized in the family of a slaveholder; it was divinely regulated among the chosen people of God, and the peculiar duties of the parties are inculcated under the Christian economy. These are facts which cannot be denied. Our argument then is this: If the Church is bound to abide by the authority of the Bible, and that alone, she discharges her whole office in regard to slavery when she declares what the Bible teaches, and enforces its laws by her own peculiar sanctions. Where the Scriptures are silent, she must be silent too. What the Scriptures have not made essential to a Christian profession, she does not undertake to make so. What the Scriptures have sanctioned, she does not condemn. To this course she is shut up by the nature of her constitution. If she had universally complied with the provisions of her charter, the angry discussions which have disgraced her courts and produced bitterness and alienation among her own children, in different countries, and in different sections of the same land, would all have been prevented.

The Abolition excitement derives most of its fury, and all its power, from the conviction which Christian people, without warrant from God, have industriously propagated, that slavery, essentially considered, is a sin. They have armed the instincts of our moral nature against it. They have given the dignity of principle to the clamours of fanaticism; and the consequence is that many churches are distracted and the country reeling under a series of assaults in which treachery to man is justified as obedience to God. According to the rule of faith which gives to the Church its being, the relation of master and slave stands on the same foot with the other relations of life. In itself considered, it is not inconsistent with the will of God – it is *not* sinful. This is as much a doctrine of Christianity as the obligation of obedience to law. The Church, therefore, cannot undertake to disturb the relation. The Bible further teaches that there are duties growing out of this relation – duties of the master and duties of the slave. The Church must enforce these duties upon her own members. Here her jurisdiction stops. As a *Church* – as the visible Kingdom of our Lord

and Saviour Jesus Christ – she must venture to interfere no
further, unless it be to repress the agitations of those who
assume to be wiser and purer than the Word of God. Those
who corrupt the Scriptures, who profanely add to the duties of the Decalogue, are no more entitled to exemption
from ecclesiastical discipline than any other disturbers of
the peace or fomenters of faction and discord. It is not a
question whether masters can be received into the communion of the saints, but it is a question whether those who
exclude them should not themselves be rejected.

We are far from insinuating that Abolitionists, *as such,*
are unfit to be members of the Church. Slavery may evidently be contemplated in various aspects – as a social arrangement, involving a distinction of classes, like oriental
caste, or European gradation of ranks – as a civil relation,
involving rights, obligations corresponding to its own nature – as a political condition, bearing upon the prosperity,
happiness and growth of communities. In any or in all
these aspects, it may be opposed upon considerations of
policy and prudence, as the despotism of Asia, the aristocracy of Europe, or the free institutions of America are opposed, without the imputation of sin upon the nature of
the relation itself. The members of the Church, as citizens
and as men, have the same right to judge of the expediency
or inexpediency of introducing and perpetuating in their
own soil this institution as any other element of their social
economy. But they transcend their sphere, and bring reproach upon the Scriptures as a rule of faith, when they go
beyond these political considerations, and condemn slavery as essentially repugnant to the will of God. They then
corrupt the Scriptures, and are exposed to the malediction

of those who trifle with the Divine Testimony.

The Southern churches have never asked their brethren in Europe or in the non-slaveholding sections of their own land to introduce slavery among them – they have never asked them to approve it as the wisest and best constitution of society. All they have demanded is, that their brethren would leave it where God has left it, and deal with it where it is found, as God has dealt with it. We insist upon it that they should not disturb the tranquillity of the State by attempting to readjust our social fabric according to their own crotchets, when we ourselves, the only parties who have a right to meddle, are satisfied with our condition. We do not recognize them as political apostles, to whom God has transferred from us the right inherent in every other people to manage their affairs in their own way, so long as they keep within the limits of the Divine Law. If we fail in our social and political organizations – if, by consequence, we lag behind in the progress of nations, we do not forfeit our right to self-government and become the minors and wards of wiser and stronger States. It is as preposterous in our Northern and European brethren to undertake to force their system upon us, or to break up our own in obedience to their notions, as it would be in us to wage a war upon theirs, on the ground that ours is better. Slavery, as a *political* question, is one in regard to which communities and States may honestly differ. But as a *moral* question, the Bible has settled it; and all we contend for is, that being a *matter of liberty*, we should not break fellowship for difference upon other grounds. If any man, however, is not content to stand by the Word of God – if any church will not tolerate the liberty wherewith Christ has made us free – that man and that church cannot be vindicated from the charge of fomenting schism. They become justly exposed to censure. He who would debar a slaveholder from the table of the Lord upon the simple and naked ground that he is a slaveholder, deserves himself to be excluded for usurping the prerogatives of Christ and introducing terms of communion which cast reproach upon the conduct of Jesus and the Apostles. He violates the very charter of the Church – is a traitor to its fundamental law.

We have been struck with three circumstances in the conduct of what may be called the Christian argument against slavery. The first is, that the principles from which, for the most part, the conclusion has been drawn, were the abstrusest of all speculations upon the vexed question of human rights, and not the obvious teachings of the Scriptures. The second is, that when the argument has been professedly taken from the Bible, it has consisted in strained applications of passages, or forced inferences from doctrines, in open violation of the law that Scripture is its own interpreter; and the third is, that duties which the Bible enjoins are not only inadequately recognized, but forced into a system of morals whose fundamental principles exclude them.

The argument from philosophy – if the dogmas of sophists upon the nature and extent of human rights can be dignified with the title of philosophy – a church court cannot admit to be authoritative, without doing violence to her own constitution. It is not denied that truth is truth, whether found in the Bible or out of it, and it is not denied that there is much truth, and truth of a most important kind, which it is not the province of revelation to teach. But then it should be remembered that this is truth with which the Church, *as such*, has nothing to do. Neither should it be forgotten, that if human speculation conducts to a moral result directly contradictory of the Scriptures, faith convicts it of falsehood, the Word of God being a surer guide than the wit of man. When the question is whether man is mistaken or the Word of God deceitful, the answer to the Church cannot be doubtful. And yet how much of the declamation against slavery, in which Christian people are prone to indulge, is founded upon principles utterly unsupported by the Scriptures? One man very complacently tells us that every man is entitled to the fruit of his own labour; and that the master, in appropriating that of the slave, defrauds him of his right. It is then denounced as a system of robbery and plunder, which every good man should labour to banish from the earth. But where is the maxim, in the sense in which it is interpreted, to be found in the Scriptures? Where, even in any respectable system of moral philosophy? Where are we taught that the labour which a man puts forth in his own person is always his, or belongs to him of right, and cannot belong to another? How does it appear that what is physically his, must be legally his? Another insists on the absolute equality of the species, and can find no arrangement in harmony with reason, but that which shall reduce the race to a stagnant uniformity of condition. But where do the Scriptures teach that an essential equality as men implies a corresponding equality of state? And who is authorized to limit the application of this sweeping principle to the sole relation of slavery? It is as much the weapon of the socialist and leveller as of the Abolitionist, and the Church cannot accept it without renounc-

ing the supremacy of the Scriptures; neither can she pro-
ceed, upon it, to excommunicate the slaveholder, without
fulminating her anathemas against the rich and the noble.
Another insists upon the essential and indestructible per-
sonality of men, and vituperates slavery as reducing human beings to the condition of chattels and of things, as if
it were possible that human legislation could convert matter into mind or mind into matter, or as if slavery were not
professedly a relation of man to man. The arguments from
this and all similar grounds can be easily answered. It will
be found, in every case, either that the principle assumed
is false in itself or distorted in its application, or that the
whole discussion proceeds on a gratuitous hypothesis in
regard to the nature of slavery. But whether they can be
answered or not, no deductions of man can set aside the
authority of God. The Bible is supreme, and as long as it
allows the institution, the Church should not dare to rebuke it. In a court of Jesus Christ we would not think of
presenting any consideration as conclusive, but "thus saith
the Lord."

But when the argument is professedly conducted from
the Bible, it is in violation of the great principle that Scripture is its own interpreter. It is notorious – it is indeed universally conceded, that no express condemnations of slavery have ever been produced from the sacred volume. The
plan is, in the absence of any thing precise and definite, to
demonstrate an incongruity betwixt the analogy and general spirit of the Bible, and the facts of slavery. Some general principle is seized upon, such as the maxim of universal benevolence, or of doing unto others as we would have
them do unto us, and brought into contrast with the degra-

dation or abuses of bondage. Or specific precepts, such as this in relation to the family are singled out, with which it is supposed slavery renders it impossible to comply. The fallacy in these cases is easily detected. The same line of argument, carried out precisely in the same way, would make havoc with all the institutions of civilized society. Indeed, it would be harder to defend from the Scriptures the righteousness of great possessions than the righteousness of slavery. The same principle which would make the master emancipate his servant, on the ground of benevolence, would make the rich man share his estates with his poor neighbours; and he who would condemn the institution as essentially and inherently evil, because it sometimes incidentally involves the disruption of family ties, would condemn the whole texture of society in the non-slaveholding States, where the separation of parents and children, of husbands and wives, is often a matter of stern necessity. But however the argument might be answered, it is enough for a Christian man, who compares Scripture with Scripture, to know that slavery is expressly excepted from the application of this or any other principles in the sweeping sense of the Abolitionists. It is not a case left to the determination of general principles – it is provided for in the law. If the Scriptures were silent in regard to it, we might appeal to analogies to aid us in reaching the will of God; but as they have mentioned the subject again and again, and stated the principles which are to be applied to it, we are shut up to these special testimonies.

Those who have been conversant with works against slavery cannot have failed to be struck with the awkward and incongruous appearance which in these works the commands of the Scriptures to masters and servants assume. They lay down principles which make slavery an utter abomination – treason to man and rebellion against God. They represent it as an enormous system of cruelty, tyranny and impiety. They make it a fundamental duty to labour for its extirpation, and yet will not venture directly and boldly – at least Christian Abolitionists – to counsel insurrection or murder; they will even repeat the commands of the Bible, as if in mockery of all their speculations. Now we ask if these commands are not forced appendages to their moral system? Are they not awkwardly inserted? The moral system of Abolitionists does not legitimately admit them; and if they were not restrained by respect for the Bible from carrying out their own doctrines, they would find themselves forced to recommend measures to the slave very different from obedience to his master. Those, accordingly, who prefer consistency to piety, have not scrupled to reject these precepts, and to denounce the book which enjoins them. They feel the incongruity betwixt their doctrines and these duties, and they do not hesitate to revile the Scriptures as the patron of tyranny and bondage. Admit the principle that slavery, essentially considered, is not a sin, and the injunctions of Scripture are plain, consistent, intelligible; deny the principle, and the Bible seems to be made up of riddles.

Such is a general view of the Christian argument against slavery. We are not conscious of having done it any injustice. We have endeavored to study it impartially and candidly; but we confess that the conviction grows upon us, that those who most violently denounce this relation have formed their opinions in the first instance independently of the Bible, and then by special pleading have endeavoured to pervert its teachings to the patronage of their assumptions. They strike us much more as apologists for the defects and omissions of the Scriptures, than as humble inquirers, sitting at the feet of Jesus to learn His will. They have settled it in their own minds that slavery is a sin; then the Bible must condemn it, and they set to work to make out the case that the Bible has covertly and indirectly done what they feel it ought to have done. Hence those peculiar features of the argument to which we have already adverted.

To this may be added a total misapprehension of the nature of the institution. Adjuncts and concomitants of slavery are confounded with its essence, and abuses are seized upon as characteristic of the very genius of the institution.

If this method of argument is to be persisted in, the consequences must ultimately be injurious to the authority of the sacred writers. Those who have not a point to gain, will easily detect the sophistry which makes the Scriptures subsidiary to Abolitionism; and if they are to receive it as a fundamental principle of morals that there can be no right to the labour of another, independently of contract, and this is the essence of slavery, they will be shut up to the necessity of denying the sufficiency and plenary inspiration of the Scriptures. Like Morell, they will take their stand upon the defective morality of the Bible, and scout the idea of any external, authoritative rule of faith. The very same spirit of rationalism which has made the Prophets and Apostles succumb to philosophy and impulse in relation to the doctrines of salvation, lies at the foundation of modern speculation in relation to the rights of man. Opposition to slavery has never been the offspring of the Bible. It has sprung from visionary theories of human nature and society – it has sprung from the misguided reason of man – it comes as natural, not as revealed truth; and when it is seen that the Word of God stands in the way of it, the lively oracles will be stripped of their authority, and reduced to the level of mere human utterances. We affectionately warn our brethren of the mischiefs that must follow from their mode of conducting the argument against us – they are not only striking at slavery, but they are striking at the foundation of our common faith. They are helping the cause of rationalism. We need not repeat that a sound philosophy must ever coincide with revelation, but what we insist upon is that in cases of conflict, the Scriptures must be supreme. Man may err, but God can never lie. If men are at liberty from their own heads to frame systems of morality, which render null and void the commandments of God, we see not why they are not equally at liberty to frame systems of doctrines which render vain the covenant of grace. If they are absolutely their own law, why not absolutely their own teachers? It is, therefore, a very grave question which *they* have to decide, who, in opposition to the example of the Apostles of our Lord, exclude masters from the communion of the saints, and from the hopes of the Gospel.

The history of the world is full of illustrations that the foolishness of God is wiser than man. There is a noble moderation in the Scriptures, upon which alone depends the stability of States and the prosperity and success of the whole social economy. It rebukes alike the indifference and torpor which would repress the spirit of improvement and stiffen society into a fixed and lifeless condition, and the spirit of impatience and innovation which despises the lessons of experience, and rushes into visionary schemes of reformation. It is in the healthful operation of all the limbs and members of the body politic that true progress consists; and he who fancies that deformities can be cured by violent and hasty amputations, may find that in removing what seemed to be only excrescences, he is inflicting a fatal stroke upon vital organs of the system. Slavery, to those who are unaccustomed to its operations, may seem to be an unnatural and monstrous condition, but it will be found that no principles can be pleaded to justify its removal which may not be applied with fatal success to the dearest interests of man. They who join in the unhallowed crusade against the institutions of the South, will have reason to repent that they have set an engine in motion which cannot be arrested until it has crushed and ground to powder the safeguards of life and property among themselves.

Deeply convinced as we are that the proper position of the Church in relation to slavery is that which we have endeavoured to present in these pages, we would earnestly and solemnly expostulate with those denominations at the North who have united in the outcry against us, and urge them to reconsider their steps in the fear of God and under the guidance of His Word. We ask them to take the Apostles as their guide. We are solemn and earnest, not only because we deplore a schism in the body of Christ, but because we deplore a schism among the confederated States of this Union. We know what we say when we declare our deliberate conviction that the continued agitation of slavery must sooner or later shiver this government into atoms; and agitated it must continue to be, unless the churches of Jesus Christ take their stand firmly and immovably upon the platform of the Bible. The people of the South ask nothing more – they will be content with nothing less. Let the churches take this position, and the people of the North will find their moral instincts rallying to the support of our Federal Constitution, and will give to the winds a policy founded on the profane insinuation that slavery is essentially a sin.

Free-soilism is nothing but the application to politics of this unscriptural dogma. If slavery be indeed consistent with the Bible, their responsibility is *tremendous,* who, in obedience to blind impulses and visionary theories, pull down the fairest fabric of government the world has ever seen, rend the body of Christ in sunder, and dethrone the Saviour in His own Kingdom. What a position for churches of Jesus Christ – aiding and abetting on the one hand the restless and turbulent designs of agitators, demagogues and radical reformers, and giving countenance on the other to a principle which, if legitimately carried out, robs the Scriptures of their supremacy, and delivers us over to the folly and madness of rationalism. Are our country, our Bible, our interests on earth and our hopes for heaven to be sacrificed on the altars of a fierce fanaticism? Are laws to be made which God never enacted – doctrines to be taught which the Apostles have condemned, and are they to be propagated and forced on men at the peril of every thing that is dear and precious? We conjure our brethren – for such we shall still call them – we conjure our brethren to pause. We do not ask them to patronize slavery – we do not wish them to change their own institutions – we only ask them to treat us as the Apostles treated the slaveholders of their day, and leave to us the liberty which we accord to them, of conducting our affairs according to our own convictions of truth and duty. We ask it of them as Christians – as professed followers of Christ; and if this reasonable demand is refused, upon them and not upon us must rest the perilous responsibility of the disasters that must inevitably follow. We are not alarmists, but slavery is implicated in every fibre of Southern society; it is with us a vital question, and it is because we *know* that interference with it cannot and will not be much longer endured, we raise our warning voice. We would save the country if we could. We would save the Constitution which our fathers framed, and we would have our children and our children's children, for countless generations, worship in the temple which our fathers reared. But this cannot be, unless our whole people shall be brought to feel that slavery is no ground of discord, and that in Christ Jesus there is neither bond nor free. Would to God that this blessed consummation could be reached!

In the mean time Christian masters at the South should address themselves with earnestness and vigor to the discharge of their solemn duties to their slaves. We would stir up their minds, not that they have been inattentive to the subject, but that they may take the more diligent heed. The most important and commanding of all their obligations is that which relates to religious instruction. Food and raiment and shelter their interests will prompt them to provide; but as the labour of the slave is expended for their benefit, they are bound, by the double consideration of justice and of mercy, to care for his soul. We rejoice that so much has already been done in imparting the Gospel to this class; and we hope that the time is not far distant when every Christian master will feel that he is somewhat in the same sense responsible for the religious education of his slaves as for the religious education of his children. The Church, too, as an organized society, should give special attention to the subject. There are many questions connected with it, which ought to be gravely and deliberately considered. We have no doubt that much effort has been uselessly expended, because injudiciously applied. Of one thing we are satisfied – their religious teachers should never be taken from among themselves. There is too great a proneness to superstition and extravagance among the most enlightened of them, to entrust them with the cure of souls. Their circumstances preclude them from the preparation and study which such a charge involves. There was wisdom in the statute of the primitive Church, which allowed none but a freeman to be a minister of the Gospel. To say nothing of the fact that their time is under the direction of their masters, we would as soon think of making ministers and elders, and organizing churches of children, as of according the same privilege to slaves. They would soon degrade piety into fanaticism, and the Church into bedlam. We rejoice that the Presbyteries of our own Synod have uniformly acted in conformity with this principle; and although our success may, by consequence, be slow, it will eventually be sure.

James Henley Thornwell (1812-1862) was born in Marlboro County, South Carolina. He graduated from South Carolina College in Columbia at the age of nineteen and briefly attended Harvard University before entering the Presbyterian ministry in 1835. He taught at South Carolina College, eventually serving as president, and went on to teach at Columbia Theological Seminary. Thornwell played a prominent role in the First General Assembly of the Presbyterian Church in the Confederate States of America in 1861. He interpreted the War Between the States as a religious conflict between orthodox Christianity on one side (the South) and atheism, communism, etc., on the other (the North).

The preceding address appeared in the *Southern Presbyterian Review*, January 1852, Vol. V, No. 3.

III

Duties of Masters
by Rev. R.S. Breck, D.D.

The incidental relations of master, growing out of the presence and servitude among us of the Black race, has been to many Southern Christians, one fixed and familiar from childhood, and in the Providence of God may so continue as long as we are in this life. The duties arising out of it, also, are of the most weighty character. The subject, therefore, becomes one of the most important that can claim the attention of the Southern Church. In it are involved the interests of three millions of dependent people, the prosperity and happiness of that large section of our country characterized by the presence of the slave, and the innocence or guilt, in the discharge or dereliction of duty, of the thousands who are bound up in this institution. The destiny of the Negro race, for wise ends, some of which we can now see, has been bound on to our own; we are constituted their guardians, their teachers, their civilizers. A large portion of our duties as a people, and as individuals, grow out of this trust. We cannot be indifferent to a subject, involving so many responsibilities, and would be inexcus-

51

able, did we permit the violence of noisy fanatics on either extreme to deter us from its consideration and discussion.

There has been, unfortunately, thrown about the subject a delicacy and reserve, which it does not naturally nor properly possess; and therefore, it has not received the attention from those immediately concerned in it, which, from its magnitude, it deserves. In one portion of the Union, there is a class of factionists, who are continually disgorging hearts of bitterness and malignity, denouncing with every opprobrious epithet of their corrupt vocabulary, all who are connected with this institution, or identified with this section of our confederacy. On the other hand, there is a class, who, repelling with intemperate zeal the charges and designs of these fanatics, oppose the discussion of the subject, and all efforts for the improvement of those who are the unfortunate occasion of its vituperation and strife. The public mind excited and feverish, and rendered unnaturally and morbidly sensitive by such distempered discussions, good men have been deterred from speaking out boldly upon the duties we owe to this race. Our duty evidently is, as we stand amid the spray and foam from the meeting of these streams, calmly, dispassionately and conscientiously to consider the whole subject. The subject, as an important department of Christian duty, must not be taken out of the hands of the ministry. If judicious men, if worthy at all to stand in the pulpit, they should be allowed to speak frankly and plainly upon it. A distinguished friend of both the South and the Black race, says of one branch of it:

I would recommend to the friends of religious instruction, not to mix it up with questions touching the civil condition of the Negroes, (1 Tim. vi: 1-8,) nor turn aside from the main work, to combat incidental evils. Time is wasted, the great cause is retarded and prejudiced. Believe in God – in His Providence – in the power of His truth and grace – and go forward. We are to lead this people unto life eternal, through the knowledge of Jesus Christ our Lord. This is the will of God – this is our duty – the great duty of the Southern church.[1]

Our course at this time is, throwing aside all the difficult and exciting questions with which the subject is embarrassed, and setting up no defence of the slave-holder, except as far as is involved in the establishment of the duties set forth, but regarding the institution as a matter of fact already existing among us, with which we are connected, to consider our duty growing out of it.

I. It will aid the master in determining many of his duties, and indeed the whole treatment of the slave, to consider and understand closely, the extent and true nature of the property he has in his fellow-being. The extent of that property is simply a claim to his services. No other right of the slave is alienated, other than that to his own labour. There is no owning by the master of the *corpus* and the *anima*. He has no such property in his slave, as he has in the ox or the swine. His soul, his head, his limbs, his heart, still belong to the slave, subject to this one restriction: of service due to another. He has a right to life, to livelihood, to happiness, to marriage, to religion, – to everything consistent with the service he is obligated to ren-

---

1. *Suggestions on the Religious Instruction of the Negroes*, by C.C. Jones, D.D.

der. With the means to secure a livelihood and religion, he has a right to be supplied out of the proceeds of his labor. Every relation in human society imposes some restraint upon personal liberty. The child possesses liberty within the parents' will.

The individual, in becoming a citizen, parts with a certain amount of personal liberty for the general good. He is free, with the restriction of the claim of the State upon him. The slave is a human being, with only the obligation of service to another. This is a fundamental distinction with writers in the defensive upon this subject. Dr. Thornwell says:

> The property of man in man, a fiction to which even the imagination cannot give consistency, is the miserable cant of those who would storm by prejudice what they cannot demolish by argument. We do not even pretend that the organs of the body can be said strictly to belong to another. The limbs and members of my servant are not mine, but his, – they are not tools and instruments which I can sport with at pleasure; but the sacred possession of a human being, which cannot be invaded without the authority of law, and for the use of which he can never be divested of his responsibility to God.
>
> Whatever control the master has over the person of the slave, is subsidiary to this right to his labor; what he sells, is not the man, but the property in his services.[2]

Dr. N. L. Rice says:

> But the gentleman tells us, that the master owns the

---

2. James Henley Thornwell, *Rights and Duties of Masters*, page 24.

man, not only the body but the soul, and that he sells the soul; what use let me ask, does the master make, or what use can he make of the slave, but to claim his labour, – his services?

By slaveholding then, I understand the claim of the master to the services of the slave with the corresponding obligation of the master....[3]

A writer in the *Princeton Review* says:

When therefore it is said that one man is the property of another, it can only mean that the one has a right to use the other as a man, but not as a brute, or as a thing. He has no right to treat him as he may lawfully treat his ox, or a tree. He can convert his person to no use to which a human being may not, by the laws of God and nature, be properly applied. When this idea of property comes to be analyzed, it is found to be nothing more than a claim of service, either for life, or for a term of years. This claim is transferable, and is of the nature of property, and is consequently liable for the debts of the owner, and subject to his disposal by will, or otherwise.[4]

The Supreme Court of Georgia says:

It is true slaves are property, and by the act of 10th of May, 1770, are declared to be personal chattels in the hands of their owners, and are alienable; but it does not thence follow, that they are mere things, horses, as was contended in argument. This property, or personal chattel, consists in *the right of governing the slave,* subject to

---

3. Dr. Nathan Lewis Rice, *A Debate on Slavery*, pages 32, 33.

4. Review of Channing, *Slavery*, 1836.

such restraints as the Legislature may impose on the master, *and of enjoying his perpetual and involuntary service.* The law has never yet ceased to consider slaves, though thus subject to the government and service of the master, as human beings, subject to its protection, and bound to obey its requirements.[5]

According to Paley's celebrated definition, slavery is "an obligation to labor for the benefit of the master, without the contract or consent of the servant."[6]

This view, taken by the master of the nature and extent of his property in him, elevates his slave from the place to which he is too often degraded, and places him before him, an immortal being, and a fellow-creature vested with sacred rights. The only claim he has upon him is for his service; when that is tendered, the obligation is discharged. Included necessarily in the right of service is the right to enforce it, – to compel obedience to reasonable commands; and if need be, to enforce it with correction; just as the State may enforce its claim upon the citizen, and the parent his claim upon the child. The master may enforce a proper respect of manner, and a regard for morals. Discipline beyond this is to be condemned, not only because it is a lack of benevolence, but because it is a violation of sacred right. The master has a right to the service of the slave; the slave has all other rights, consistent with this and with the laws of society. It is the bounden duty of the master to respect those rights and as the claim he holds

---

5. The Judges in Convention, forming the highest judicial tribunal in the State; in the case of the *State vs. Philpot.*

6. *Moral Philosophy,* Book iii, Chapter 3.

upon his slave is so large a portion of that usually esteemed by men, to endeavor to promote his happiness, in the enjoyment of all other rights, remaining and pertaining to him. (Col. iv: 1).

II. This relation is to be regarded as belonging to the family, coming under the same general policy and benevolent discipline, regulating the other family relations. It is not so intimate or tender as that of husband and wife, or parent and child, but the obligations growing out of it are not less sacred; and while not appealing with the same power to the affections, there is yet that mutual dependence, that permanence, constancy, and intimacy of association, that require its admission within this pale of hallowed ties. Upon an examination of the Word of God, and of the arguments outside of Bible history, by which slavery is usually defended, we believe that only in this light is it capable of defence. To deprive a human being of so important a right, which leaves him in utter dependence for a worldly provision, and for the security of all his other rights, without throwing over him the protection of the family, cannot be justified upon any grounds. The complexity and multiplicity of the engagements of men, demanding a division of labour, may require this character in the family to perform the humbler and more menial labor; but the moment the relation is placed upon any other ground than that of convenience and mutual benefit, or withdrawn from the pale of family ties, you erect a pure despotism, no more capable of defence than the serfdom of Russia, which binds the boar perpetually to the soil, subject to the disposal of the crown, or some petty despot; and not so easily defended, as the vassalage of feudal times, which secured to the serving class protection, so valuable in a barbaric age.

Among the servants of the Hebrews, were three classes. The first, were those rendering voluntary service, and receiving wages, or hired servants.[7] The second class were those sold for pauperism,[8] or debt,[9] or crime,[10] or children sold by parents,[11] or Hebrews ransomed from Gentile masters,[12] and serving without wages for a term of years. These were Hebrews, and always were restored to freedom at the jubilee; so that in no case, could they serve longer than six years.[13] The third class, were bondmen, or slaves, held in perpetual servitude. These were bought of the heathen nations around,[14] or captives taken in war,[15] and could not be Hebrews,[16] except in a case definitely stated of the voluntary abandonment of freedom.[17]

Now, this last class became identified with the family, passed under the same laws and discipline with its other members, were circumcised just as the children of the master; thus, by virtue of their connection with the family, in-

---

7. Deut. xxiv: 14, 15.

8. Lev. xxv: 39, 40.

9. 2 Kings iv: 1.

10. Ex. xxii: 3.

11. Ex. xxi: 7.

12. Lev. xxv: 47-54.

13. Ex. xxi: 2.

14. Lev. xxv: 44-46.

15. Deut. xx: 14.

16. Lev. xxv: 42.

17. Ex. xxi: 5, 6.

troduced into the Jewish Church.[18] These bond-men, observe, were heathen; but we find no such requisition or provision for heathen *hired servants,* and it is clear that some of their hired servants were heathen.[19] The number of these bondmen held by the patriarchs was very great; and now the number of such servants owned by a single individual may be large; and in a country where slavery is established, from their multiplication, or the diminution of the personal wants of the family, they may not be literally within the bounds of the family; still the relation was, and must be, predicated upon the idea of the family; and when these servants are removed from the person of the master, it must be regarded as a separation of the family.

In the New Testament, the grouping together in several places of the relations of the family, including those of master and servant, is remarkable and in confirmation of this view of these relations. As in Colossians iii: 18-32, and iv: 1: "Wives submit yourselves unto your husbands.... Husbands love your wives.... Children obey your parents in all things.... Fathers provoke not your children to anger.... Servants obey in all things your masters according to the flesh.... Masters give unto your servants that which is just and equal."

If these views are correct, and they seem to be fair inferences from these passages of Scripture, then it elevates the slave still higher. Not only does he stand before the intelligent master an immortal fellow-being, clothed with rights of the most sacred character, but he is a member of

---

18. Gen. xvii: 12, 13.

19. Deut. xxiv: 14.

his family; in virtue of the paramount claim upon him, entitled to its protection, provision, sympathy and whatever of general benevolence and kindness prevails towards its other members; ever, however, with a due reference to his position. He is the lowest member, but still a member. And we verily believe that so long as he discharges his obligation faithfully, next to the great primary relations of the family, his is the great claim on earth upon the master.

III. Upon these two considerations, a third naturally arises, that it is the duty of masters, by all proper and lawful means, to seek to promote the welfare of this class of our fellow-beings, and to secure to them the greatest amount of happiness their condition will admit. We do not know but that with the conscientious performance of the master's duty, they may be made just as happy a class as any other; for if they have peculiar trials, they escape many of the cares that harass our minds; but this only renders the injunction the more important. Our principle should be, *amelioration*, – the softening down of the harsher features in their condition, and the removal of all unnecessary evils. As we look upon the institution as it exists in our midst, we would be blind not to perceive that there are evils connected with it to the Blacks. There are evils connected with all the relations of life: that of husband and wife, parent and child, apprentice and master; and from its very nature, this is more liable to abuse than any other. But most of the evils of slavery among us are not inseparable from the relation. A faithful discharge of this general duty may remove many of them.

There are several ways in which we are to aid in the advancement of the happiness of the slave race. We are to do it by a proper performance of duty to those in our own families, – providing them with suitable apartments, clothing, food and fuel; affording them sufficient relaxation; respecting their relations among themselves; instructing them; striving to elevate their moral character; and stimulating them by kindness. We are to do it by lending our influence to form a just and healthy public sentiment, that will bear down any who may treat their slaves with indecency, or inhumanity. We are to do it by upholding strict church discipline upon all members who grossly neglect or violate their duty to their slaves. And we are to do it by aiding to secure the passage of laws for the protection of Blacks against masters who have no regard for public sentiment. There has been an evident advance upon this subject in the last few years. Masters generally are more mindful of the comfort and happiness of their slaves. There is a much sounder, juster public sentiment respecting the exercise of many of the legal rights of masters. The slave is more protected by law from cruelty in most of the slaveholding States. In one respect, his privileges have been curtailed in many of the States by the cruel work of Abolitionists, in the circulation of their incendiary publications. To protect the Blacks and the Whites against these, laws have been enacted, prohibiting the learning of slaves to read; and even these in some of the States exist only upon the statute book, a mere dead letter. Upon the whole, there has been an advance in legislation, rendering the condition of this portion of our population more easy and comfortable. But a great deal remains yet to be done. We say it with candor and sincerity. Let us not be swerved from our duty by the cries and vituperation of fanatics, but let us think and act like Christian men, sensible of our obligations. Our duty as Southern Christians is to press forward in this work of amelioration, – establishing, upon a firmer basis, the happiness of this people, and relieving them from the evils not necessary, or inseparable from their condition as slaves.

IV. The peculiarity of the marriage relation among the slaves, as the most prolific source of the evils of their present condition, claims the especial consideration of the Christian master. It is urged by Abolitionists, that slavery necessarily and *per se* vitiates and destroys marriage, or renders it impossible. We quote from Mr. Blanchard, as representing their views and reasoning upon this subject:

> Slavery, adjudges slaves unmarried, and incapable of marriage. It holds the slave pair in separation, ready to be sold apart. He (his opponent Dr. Rice,) tells us, but they are vain words, that the husband and wife are not separated in slavery, unless the master chooses to part them. But if I come to own a man and his wife, are they not already separated so far as the nuptial tie bound them, and ready to be sold apart whenever I will to sell them? Suppose I sell the woman, and the purchaser goes to get her: has he anything to do but to lead her off? Is there anything to be done to separate her from her husband? Obviously nothing. She ceased, by the theory of slavery, to be her husband's *wife,* when she became my *woman.* The property principle is stronger, in law and practice, than the marriage principle, and prevails over it.

The error of this reasoning, is found in a gross neglect of the distinction between the absurd form of words, "property of man in man," and property in his services, and in an unwarranted abrasion of a right, because it is trampled upon, or not defined by law. No man can have any other claim upon his slave and his wife, than for their service; and the right of permanent marriage relation belongs to them, and is contemplated by the institution, in any benevolent or just view of it, though it be not respected by a ruffian, or protected by legislative enactment. We need not say to any just or pure-minded man that the slaves are married – married in the sight of high heaven, and in the esteem of good men, – where with the rites of religion, they have pledged their truth or fidelity. We freely confess, however, that there is an evil, in that the legal definitions of slavery, and of the rights and duties of masters, in the acts of our legislatures, and the utterances of our courts, do not conform perfectly to the true nature of the institution, as recognised by the virtuous and the good; and, also, in that these higher and more benevolent views, founded in natural justice, do not prevail among all the holders of slaves. Whilst this reasoning of Abolitionists is false, it is sufficient to suggest to us, that there is a real evil upon which it is founded, and that we are very much at fault upon this head. The marriage relation of the Blacks is not sufficiently respected by Blacks themselves, or by the Whites; nor is it sufficiently protected by the law of the land. Its binding, permanent obligation, the majority of slaves do not comprehend. They feel a freedom to change their relations at will, or at least with every change of residence. The result of this is, a very low standard of morality among them. Three-fourths of our cases of church discipline among them arise from this source. For the proof of this, we may appeal to the sessional records of any church, which has a considerable coloured membership. It is very evident that a reform is needed. This reform must commence with individuals and families. We must respect ourselves, their marriage relations, – encourage them to form them, – make sacrifices to keep them united, – and encourage them to seek the sanction and solemnities of our holy religion in their marriages. Duty will also carry us further, to seek, as far as practical, to keep together their children. A just public sentiment is forming, and, to a limited extent, already exists, that will not tolerate the man, who, for considerations of a mere pecuniary nature, tears asunder those bound together by the most sacred of earthly ties, – who sets a few dollars against the happiness and sacred right of two human beings. This public sentiment we are to encourage and promote by all judicious means.

The Church, as an organization, has a work to do in this reform. It must look closely to the relations of all this class in their communion. Its ministers must perform for them, as for their other parishioners, the marriage service, and baptize their children, as they baptize the children of the Whites. But there are many unfortunately in our land who have the control of the happiness of human beings, who cannot appreciate high moral considerations, who are indurated not to fear public sentiment, and who cannot be reached by the Church. To protect against such masters, the authority of the State is required. We believe that a law prohibiting the separation of husband and wife, except for crime, by a greater distance than five or ten miles, would secure the best interests of the master as well as the slave, and would be sustained by public sentiment in most or all of the States of the South. It might have the effect to embarrass this kind of property under certain circumstances, and for the time; it would result, however, in the division of servants more according to families; and by the increased happiness and morality of the slaves, would more than compensate the masters. A gratifying evidence of the advance of public sentiment upon this subject, is furnished in the recommendation by the Governor of Alabama, in his last annual message to the legislature, of the passage of more stringent laws to prevent the separation of mothers from children under ten years of age, and to secure the permanence of the relation of husband and wife.[20] We trust the time is not distant when in every State in which this institution exists, the permanence of the marriage relation among slaves will be a matter not of caprice, – not merely resting upon the benevolence or the moral sense of the master, – but a matter of law.

V. But our greatest and most difficult duty, growing out of our relations to this people, is to supply them with the proper religious instruction. Simple benevolence would establish this duty. God has brought the heathen to our very door. Did we sustain no relation to them, we could not turn away from them; humanity would cry aloud against us: but sustaining the relation we do, this has become, not a matter of benevolence, but of justice. We owe it to this people to give them the Gospel; they have bought it by their labour, which, given to us, leaves them without the means of procuring it. It is the great palliative of their

---

20. With the legislation of the State of Alabama, the writer is not familiar; he is not informed as to the action upon this recommendation.

condition, considered with reference to their removal from their native, heathen soil, that they have, by the change, come into possession of the knowledge of the true religion. It is our duty to see that they receive the full measure of this benefit, so far as respects the enjoyment of the means of grace. How are we to supply them with suitable religious instruction, is a question of magnitude, which is proposed for our solution. A portion of the answer is plain and easy; but there are problems of great difficulty in the complete determination of the question.

It is the duty of heads of families to provide for the instruction of domestics in their homes. This should be done by reading to them the Scriptures, with simple comments and explanations, and the use of some easy catechism. Especially should the domestics be gathered in at family prayer; and the service should ever have a reference to them. If their number is large, they should still be provided for. Any one who can keep near him more servants than can be accommodated in a single apartment of the house, is able to construct a room for the purpose. The Sabbath school, in regions where it is practicable, is an important means in supplying this instruction. This agency is practicable, especially in towns and villages, and in communities where planters are resident with their slaves. But, unfortunately, in some sections where the Blacks are congregated in greatest numbers, there is an absence of those capable of instructing them. May we not hope that the time is approaching, when a sufficient knowledge of the Holy Scriptures, to instruct in a school on the Sabbath those whose labours he superintends during the week, will be deemed by the enlightened planter a necessary qualification in the manager of slaves?

But the preaching of the Gospel has been ordained by the Head of the Church, and the Author of salvation, to be the great instrumentality in the religious instruction and the conversion of men. With this means of grace, therefore, it is our bounded duty to supply this people. The preaching we give them should be something more than the noisy, and often unintelligible harangues they hear from those of their own colour. To leave them to such, would be to leave the blind to be led by the blind. It is rarely that one is found among them at all qualified to be a religious instructor to others. Their very ignorance demands a greater intelligence, to discriminate and adapt communications to their capacities. Besides, they do not entertain for one of their own colour the respect or veneration that will render his ministrations useful to any great extent, and especially, that will qualify him for administering discipline authoritatively. The general dependance of the race is exhibited in their turning to the Whites for authority in religious, as well as in temporal matters. "The parasite has clung to the wall of adamant." However the aspiring ones among them may feel, the masses look upon the White man as their natural religious teacher; and if he will go to them, with a simplicity that brings him to a level with their comprehension, in places where they are not embarrassed by the presence of their superiors, and with services in which they are capable of engaging, they will gather around him with interest and affection.

The best mode of securing to them intelligent preaching, is a subject deserving the earnest consideration of the Church. Among the modes adopted, there is one which is being abandoned in many of our towns and cities, of providing them seats in the house with the Whites. Against this, there lies the very serious objection, that the preaching and other services in our churches, is not adapted to their mental organization or measure of intelligence. They require a simplicity of preaching, which it is the prerogative of only a high order of genius to combine with an elevation and finish, necessary to retain an intelligent congregation in the present day. Singing is a part of Divine worship, in which, when adapted to them, they engage with great delight: but we are refining the thing away to such a degree, that even the intelligent worshipper, with a book in his hand, is unable to take part in, or appreciate it. What devotion can the poor unlettered Negro find in it? The language even of our prayers, is generally so far above them, they are unable to engage in this part of the service intelligently. This incongeniality of our services, mainly, with the restraining influence of the presence of the Whites, the operation of the social feeling in drawing them to congregations of their own colour, and the desire for a worship, some part of which may be performed by themselves, has driven them away from our churches. So, if deemed the most effective and appropriate means of furnishing them preaching, this would not now be practicable.

After relinquishing this, and the hope of supplying them with adequate preaching by those of their own colour, the only method left us is to follow them to their separate place of worship with the White preacher. There let them find the gratification of their strong social feeling, and let all the services be ordered with reference to them alone. Let the subjects of preaching be of the simplest and

most practical character, and the simplest, yet most striking illustrations be studied. Let prominence be given to
exposition of Scripture, and to singing, for which they have
a passion, and the finest natural taste. Let whatever talent
any of them may possess for exhortation, or public prayer,
be drawn out in informal and social meetings. Let their
taste be consulted, in all non-essential things pertaining to
the congregation, the mode of conducting the devotion in
singing, – with or without a choir, – the arrangement and
improvement of the house, and all matters about which
they may manifest feeling or interest. Give them the feeling
of property in the house and all its services, – a home feeling that, with many clustering associations, will bind them
to their place of worship.

The mode of ecclesiastical organization proper to be
adopted among this people, that will secure efficiency and
preserve the features of our church government, presents
an interesting and important but difficult question for solution by our Southern Church. There are three general plans
which have claims to our consideration. The White pastor
and a separate worship for the Blacks enter into each of
them. The first, is that now generally adopted in our
churches, of including the colored communicants under the
same organization with the Whites, committing the oversight of both congregations to the same bench of elders.
The Church will, no doubt, but slowly, if ever, relinquish
this plan. And yet, it evidently lacks efficiency without the
addition of a class of unofficial functionaries from among
the Blacks. The expression by its committee, of the general
sense of the Presbytery of Charleston, elicited by a conference of its members on this subject at its late meeting, cor-

rectly sets forth the difficulty to be obviated, and the necessity of this addition:

> On the whole, in view of the fact that there is, from the nature of the case, a want of free and unreserved communication in spiritual matters between the two races, that there are times when, and situations in which, the Blacks are inaccessible by the Whites, and that their circumstances and conduct can only be intimately known by men of their own color, – it appeared to be the general judgment of Presbytery, that a class of functionaries should be chosen from among themselves, whose office it shall be, to assist the pastor or missionary in the discharge of those duties, which he cannot with propriety or efficiency perform in person.

Those who have had experience with congregations of coloured people, know how to appreciate the difficulty and the necessity here expressed. The difficulty can no doubt be in some degree removed by adopting this measure, which seems to have met the approval of the greater portion, and the more experienced members of Presbytery. But this difficulty removed, there are others, though not of as formidable nature. Is it not found to be the case, that the care of a single congregation, especially if it be a large one, is amply sufficient for one session? And then, there are many more cases of discipline in a coloured congregation proportionately to number, than in a White congregation. The demands upon the time of a session in order to the proper government of the Blacks where they are numerous, are far greater than are made in attention to the other interests of the church. Perhaps, if all our sessions were what they should be, all these interests could be properly attended to. But where we are aiming at practical results, in a matter as difficult as that of preserving order and discipline among this people, we must make large allowance for difficulties in the way of the efficiency of Sessions. The difficulty of bringing men together, who are engaged closely in different avocations, and of receiving that amount of attention requisite for this double work, together with the strong probability that if any interests are to be neglected they will be those of the coloured portion of the congregation, are sufficient perhaps to indicate the propriety of the division of this labor. If the Session be enlarged, so as to be able to assign this portion of the duties to a committee, the responsibility and the action are not at last removed from the Session as a whole; and to make this enlargement, it may be necessary to introduce men into the Session, who would not be acceptable elders to the White communicants, although entirely competent for the latter duties alone; or the body may be so much enlarged, as to interfere with its efficiency. In addition to this, it is worth while to consider the influence upon the Blacks, of the feeling that they are a mere attachment to another congregation, without being, in point of fact, a part of it, and the lack of that interest which the feeling that an officer or a thing is one's own, generally inspires. Notwithstanding these difficulties, it may be found by the wisdom of the church, that the present organization, with the selection of watchmen or leaders to assist the pastor and session, is upon the whole, the best.

The second plan of organization, is to create separate churches of Blacks with ordained elders of their own colour. A proposition was made to the Synod of Georgia, at its session in Savannah two years since, and by that body discussed and rejected, to authorize the formation of such a church in a missionary region, remote from any Presbyterian congregation. The evils of this plan are too obvious to require of us any extended notice of them, the want of judgment which characterizes the Blacks, their lack of intelligence, their inconstancy, and easy elation upon promotion to authority, the embarrassment from the want of harmony between the relations it would create, and their social and civil condition, and the real impossibility of a slave's performing all the functions of a ruling elder. These must be at once decisive.

The third plan, which seems to us to promise the greatest degree of efficiency with the fewest difficulties, and perfect harmony with our system of government, is to organize the Blacks with judicious and active Whites as elders, into separate churches, regularly connected with Presbytery. It would contribute greatly to the efficiency of this plan, also, though it is adapted to the production of a much stronger bond of union between the coloured people and their Session than can exist under the first, to add the watchmen. Let this Session be composed of men, not only judicious but devoted, who will at least, by turns, attend the meetings of their charge. The church thus constituted might be placed under the pastoral care of the minister of the White congregation, if all the services of a minister could not be secured.

The advantages of this plan would be: the deeper interest and greater sense of responsibility on the part of the eldership, from the more specific duty imposed upon them; an undivided attention to bestow upon the affairs of the church; a larger personal knowledge of the wants of the congregation; a stronger sympathy between the elders and people; more freedom on the part of the Blacks to communicate with the Session; and a direct representation of this portion of our population in our Church courts. The last consideration, we regard one of great importance. The presence of elders representing coloured congregations, would be an interesting and valuable element in our Presbyteries and Synods, and would secure attention to the spiritual interests of this large and dependent class of our people. Their religious instruction is already beginning to receive much attention from our Presbyteries, but how much would our interest in them be heightened, and how much less likely to forget our duty, if we had their representatives sitting in our midst, and standing upon the floor, urging their claims! This is a subject which should share largely our attention as courts of the Church. Next to the conversion to God of the freemen of this country, our brethren according to the flesh, the enlightenment and salvation of the Black race among us, and in our very homes, is the highest and most important end to which our thoughts and labors can be directed. Judged irrespective of the magnitude of the objects, perhaps the Blacks have the greatest claims upon us. They are dependent upon us; they are without the intelligence or the means of supplying themselves with the Gospel. And viewing the relation as one of reciprocal advantage, of the duties arising on our side, it certainly seems this one of giving them the Gospel should have great prominence, and be esteemed especially sacred.

The whole subject of our duty to this people, is one of

vast importance. A solemn and fearful responsibility is imposed upon us, through the relation we sustain to them. Their happiness and their salvation are largely committed to us. At the great tribunal, the bar of God, we have to account for our trust. The subject deserves to be studied in all its bearings, and to be discussed freely and prayerfully.

❧

R. S. Breck was an ordained Southern Presbyterian minister and served as Chancellor at Central University at Richmond, Kentucky.

The preceding address was taken from a sermon on the Fifth Commandment, and originally appeared in this form in the *Southern Presbyterian Review*, October 1854, Vol. VIII, No. 4.

IV

The Religious Instruction of Our Colored Population
by Rev. E. T. Baird, D.D.

The religious instruction of our servants is a matter of such importance, and uniformly excites so much interest among Christians at the South, that we feel sure we shall obtain ready and solemn attention to what we now feel constrained to say on that momentous subject. From their peculiar relation to our colored population, the churches of Jesus Christ in the Southern States have the duty devolving on them of attending to this interest. With reference to it as your spiritual overseers – exercising a watchful care over that part of His fold which the Great Shepherd hath committed to us – we desire to address you in the fear of the Lord.

We, as Presbyterians, are especially bound to consider these duties, and to act with reference to them. Our land has been kept in agitation, both in Church and State, by mad politicians and fanatical reformers, these many years; and now we see several of the leading churches of our land rent asunder – divided by geographical lines – and the pil-

75

lars of the Republic are made to tremble. But God has mer-
cifully preserved our church from all this storm of passion
and fanaticism – and we are still, thanks to His great
name, a united church, in faith, in worship, and in labor –
united in all the work and duty belonging to us as a Christian church. Doubtless many and varying opinions are held
among us, North and South, on the difficult subject of Negro slavery; but, in everything pertaining to our duties and
calling as a church of the Lord Jesus, we are perfectly
united. And hence, our Annual Assemblies are freed from
all scenes of excitement; and, as a denomination, we have
been able to address ourselves to the great business of
preaching the Gospel, which is our high calling, both to the
free and the bond – both at home and abroad, with abundant evidences of the Divine favor, and with increasing
manifestations of popular confidence.

Nor has our own branch of the Church Catholic as
such, nor the Southern portions of it in particular, been
wholly remiss, in reference to the religious care of our servants. The General Assembly, by repeated injunctions and
annual inquiry, has kept the subject fresh before the conscience of the church – many of our best and ablest ministers have devoted themselves, in whole or in part, to special labor for the salvation of these people – and our Southern Churches, Presbyteries and Synods, are yearly showing
an increased interest and watchfulness in reference to it.
Among our own churches, this Presbytery is glad to know
and to record the fact, that religious privileges are enjoyed
by the servants in very many places in common with their
masters, such as to leave them without excuse. And several
of our churches report a large colored membership, even

equal to, or larger than, the membership of Whites. But we are painfully aware, at the same time, that in many places, even among our own people, in reference to this duty, there is great neglect, arising doubtless, in some measure, from a lack of interest in religion itself; but, also, in great part, we fear, from a too low or an inadequate estimate of the true responsibilities of masters and churches in reference to the religious care of our servants.

Nothing is more clear from the Sacred Scriptures, than that a man's servants are considered as a part of his own household, for the social and moral, as well as economical care of whom, he is responsible to God and man. The father of the faithful himself was especially commended, because he was faithful in training his household to worship and serve God. And this particular commendation is so given, as to carry with it an assurance of the Divine blessing on those who follow the footsteps of the venerable patriarch in this respect – and, by immediate and necessary consequence, to denounce a curse on those who neglect this solemn responsibility. Since the master stands in this particular relation to his servants – to the law and the Commonwealth he is responsible for their social and physical welfare – and to God and His Church, for their moral care and their religious instruction. As the Commonwealth holds the master responsible for the conduct of his servants, and places the control of them in his hands for that end – by very necessity, as well as by the law of Christ, their religious instruction is lodged in his hands, insomuch that, unless he provide for it in some way, it becomes an utter impossibility. And hence, the higher you make the rights of the master, whether viewed in the light of God's law, or that of the State, the more stringent become his obligations, and the more fearful his responsibilities for the moral elevation and the religious education of the servant.

The scriptural argument for slavery, as an institution recognized by God, has no force the moment we deny these moral and religious duties; but, in so far as we recognize the scriptural argument, it carries with it a tremendous power in enforcing on the conscience of the master these heavy and tremendous obligations for which he must render an account to God. And we here desire to say, as a Presbytery, that we are glad our fellow-citizens of all classes in the South are now more and more disposed to examine the subject in its scriptural aspects, and to found the mutual duties of the relation on scriptural grounds. For that places it on such a basis that every master must see and feel these obligations, and cannot preserve a good conscience before God or man unless he discharge them. It is a good thing, therefore, for the Southern Church – a good thing for the master – aye, and a glorious thing for the servant, that this is becoming among us the popular way of examining this whole question, and of determining the duties and mutual obligations as well as moral responsibilities arising out of the relation. And one of the chief purposes we have in view in addressing you, is to bring before your minds afresh some of these weighty duties in all the force of their moral and scriptural bearing.

1. The true scriptural idea of slavery is that of the patriarchal relation. This is abundantly taught in the history of the old patriarchs – in the economy of the Jews – and in the apostolical epistles. The master is essentially the head of the household in all relations – the head of his wife – the

head over his children – and the head over his servants. His duties as such, under the patriarchal dispensation, made him the priest of the family – under the Mosaic economy as such, he made provision for their introduction into the Jewish Church, and for their religious care – and, as a necessary consequence, under the Christian dispensation he is placed under an analogous relation, requiring from him corresponding duties, in securing them the benefits of the Christian Church.

2. Slavery, as an institution of society, is simply a form of government; and is a safe and valuable institution just in so far as it is administered with equity. This principle the Apostle teaches, with great clearness and force, when he commands masters to render unto their servants that which is just and equal; and when he assures them of their direct accountability to God. Servants are essentially the poor of the land – usually, in the history of the human family, we find that they have been taken from the more ignorant and depraved tribes of men, and subjected to those who were in all respects their superiors; and this has emphatically been the case among us.

Government has for its object the restraining of the passions of bad men, the protection and defence of the ignorant and the helpless, and the maintenance of the essential rights of all. The master, in a system, of servitude such as prevails with us, must hence occupy a two-fold relation to his servants, viz: that of the parent to train, to provide for, to protect and to instruct them; and that of the magistrates to control, restrain and punish them. If all these duties are discharged aright, it is fraught with untold blessings to the ignorant and the helpless, and becomes to them a safe and sure means of their progressive elevation in the moral and intellectual scale. But so, also, if these same duties are neglected, or if the power put into the hands of the master for the good of his servant be abused by him, the institution becomes, on the other hand, a source of immeasurable evil to the master and the servant, and renders the whole system dangerous as a very volcano, ready to burst with fearful and destructive violence upon us. Happily for us, in our great and noble Commonwealth, the law clearly recognizes and abundantly enforces, by solemn sanctions, these great principles, so far as the physical well-being and the civil rights of our servants are concerned; but those other duties, pertaining to the spiritual welfare of the servant, it leaves, as it were by necessity, to the master and the Church of Christ.

3. Servitude does not have for its end nor object the degrading of the slave as a human being, but rather his elevation. Under our laws, and under every just government, all his rights as a human being are clearly confessed; his rights as a member of the Commonwealth to its protection, and his responsibility as a constituent part of it, are all clearly defined and distinctly embodied in the law. Obedience to law, and obedience to lawful authority, are entirely consistent with the highest development of the human faculties, where the laws infringe on none of the moral rights of man, and where authority is enforced with justice and equity. The most noble qualities of our nature shine out beautifully and touchingly in the life of David, while he was servant of a most unrighteous master; and, among the noblest specimens of the human character, in the lofty dignity of the truest manliness, stands forth Eliezer of Damas-

cus, the steward of Abraham's household. The reason of this, in the case of David was that his heart was full of the fear of the Lord; and, in the case of Eliezer, because his master was a man of faith, who trained his household to worship and serve God. Among us, also, may be found some noble specimens of the true and cultivated gentleman; and also of humble, exemplary and godly Christians, who were born and raised to servitude, but surrounded by Christian influences and example. But, on the other hand, neglect, evil example, unjust and cruel treatment, degrade both the master and the slave, and justly bring down on the offender the wrath of God, and the condign punishment of the State. For the well-being of the Commonwealth, as well as for the true interests of the citizen and the subject, it is absolutely essential that every member of the State, of whatever condition, should not only feel his responsibility, but should also have a conscious assurance of his own rights. The knowledge that he enjoys this protection at the hands of his master, and from the State, elevates the servant as a moral being – binds him more strongly in attachment to the household of which he forms a part – and prepares the way for further and more enlarged efforts for his spiritual good.

4. The true idea of all government, of whatever kind, is the good of the governed – a maxim which lies at the basis of all true government, which is inwrought into the theory and structure of our American constitutions, and which is universally conceded. This same principle the Apostle teaches, in enjoining obedience to rulers, when he declares that they are "ministers of God to thee for good;" and, also, when he enjoins masters to do that which is just

and equal. They, on their part, are commanded to be obe-
dient servants, in view of their accountability to God; but
this injunction is immediately connected with the exhortation to masters already referred to. And so the one exhortation and the other harmonize beautifully in their effects,
when both parties discharged their duties in God's fear.
The master has the control of the person, and enjoys the
labor of his servant, in return for his personal care, in free-
ing him from want, providing him the things necessary and
convenient, protecting him in the enjoyment of all his personal and moral rights, and securing to him Gospel privileges.

5. The moral law is the absolute rule of moral duty,
and so also it is the charter of human rights. It is the right
of every human being, prince, subject and citizen, parents
and children, masters and servants, to obey the law of
God. No government in the commonwealth or in the
household, can be called any thing less than unrighteous,
which denies to any of God's intelligent creatures the right
of obeying these moral commands, or which inhibits the
free exercise of that right. One of the very highest duties of
the master, in rendering to his servants that which is just
and equal, is to secure for them the right and opportunity
to worship and obey God, to protect them in the free exercise, and to encourage them in the constant practice thereof.

6. The responsibilities of the master are analogous to
those of the parent. But in some respects they are more
fearful and more abiding. Children and servants alike are
dependent on the parent and master respectively for all
moral culture and religious opportunities – and on these

last, instrumentally, depends in a great measure their salvation. But children, by the law of God and the land, when they are at their majority, are freed from the law of the family, and have to sustain a personal responsibility thereafter. Whereas, the servant's minority is ended only at death, and the responsibility of the master ends only at the grave of his servant. Great and tremendous, therefore, are his duties, – and, if unfaithful, awful must be his account at the judgment bar.

In view of principles such as these derived from the Word of God, and from the very nature of the relation of master and servant, how momentous are the obligations of the master? In the Providence of God, he has the control of moral and accountable beings, who must appear with him at the judgment bar, to be sentenced to heaven or to hell. How fearful a thing is an immortal soul? and oh! what interests cluster around it, as we consider its nature which bears the image of God; or when we contemplate its destiny, as an inhabitant of heaven, or as a prisoner in the gulf of perdition. And yet in all your dealings with your servants, you are impressing them for eternity; and, in every view we take of the subject, whether derived from the Divine Word or from the principles of government and the nature of the relation, we find ourselves brought into contact with immortal and accountable beings, whom, by our efforts and influence, with God's blessing, we may lead to heaven – and whom, by that same influence misdirected, we may consign to hell.

Look, brethren, at your duty in the light of eternity, and contemplate it with reference to what you are to them and they are to you. We are addressing ourselves to you, who profess to love the Lord, and who are the members of our churches. The Gospel, by which you hope to be saved, is a Gospel of love – its great principle is, love to God and love to man. And in it we are asked, how is it possible for us to love God, whom we have not seen, if we love not our brother whom we have seen? To make this principle a little more specific in its application, our servants are bone of our bone, and flesh of our flesh. The Saviour Jesus, who died for us, died for them. How can we love Christ, and yet be destitute of love for our servants; and how can you, who are masters, refuse to exert yourselves for their salvation? The older ones gathered around your cradles and welcomed you into the world with joy in your nestling infancy; the younger ones were the friends, the companions and playmates of your childhood – all of them have participated both in your joys and in your sorrows. When you have wept at the graves of your kindred, they have wept with you; and when you shall be gathered to your fathers, among the sincerest mourners at your graves will be your own servants. How can you love Christ, and not love to give your servants, who are your best and most attached friends, the Gospel of His love? And oh! how dare you think of that day and hour, when you shall be summoned yourselves by the Great Master, to give an account of your stewardship, and leave undone this most important part of your duty. And if it shall be so that, by God's great mercy, you shall yourselves be saved as by fire, how think you will you appear at the judgment seat, if it shall then be seen that your servants are lost through your default? Fearful, brethren, are the responsibilities of the master.

But, aside from all these weighty and solemn obligations, derived from the Divine Word, the nature of the relation between you and them is such that, wherever generosity dwells in the human bosom, one of the most natural and beneficent effects of its presence would seem to be, to lead the master – not sluggishly, but gladly – to obtain every available religious privilege for his servants. They attend on you from your cradles to the grave – they sang the nursery song over you as the nurses of your childhood – they led your feet in your boyish sports, and they have been your servitors in the midst of the more weighty cares of your maturer life. The labor which they have discharged for you has been the source of your comforts and the increase of your wealth. And now, as they have served you in the things that are carnal, think not it is a small thing, indeed, that you should make them partakers of your spiritual things? What answer does the generosity of your nature give? They have souls to be saved or to be lost – assuredly to be lost if you make no provision for them – but which may be saved, by God's mercy, if you bring the Gospel to them. Surely the voice of humanity calls loud to you, and unites with every prompting of beneficent hearts to secure the Gospel of salvation for the servants of your households.

The ways of Providence are very mysterious, and very great. What were the wise and holy purposes which God had in view, in suffering the African slave trade to be established three centuries ago, we are not allowed to say – but very manifestly the presence of these people among us brings on us of the South very high duties and responsibilities. The ultimate salvation of the tribes of Ham doubtless was one great end – and, already, new choirs are formed in heaven from these people, saved from barbarism and heathen degradation, unto the praise of God's grace. And the ultimate working of this whole institution of African slavery, as its past history among us abundantly shows, is to result in the moral elevation and the Christianization of these people – which, indeed, we apprehend to be the purpose of all the work Christ is doing in the world with reference to its various nations and tribes. You, then, who are masters, are co-workers with Christ unto this end, if ye be found faithful; and at the great day your crown of rejoicing shall be in proportion to your fidelity.

The influence of the Gospel on the character of your servants, and on the condition of society among us, we may expect to be good and valuable in proportion to our own fidelity. It is that conservative and life-giving power which God employs for elevating and saving the nations of men. The progress of Christianity among ourselves manifestly has exerted a great influence on the state of civilization among our White population, and all the conditions of social life with us are a vast improvement on what we know they were in the earlier days of our country. But when we look for a single moment at the condition of our slaves, and compare it with what they were when they first came among us, barbarians and heathens from Africa, we are constrained to cry out: What hath not the Lord wrought for them? To-day they are as far superior to their savage ancestors as we are superior to them. So, also, this advancing civilization among them, sanctified by the spirit of Christianity, has done much to ameliorate the whole institution of slavery, and to open the way for the relaxing of many of the rigorous regulations incident to a state of barbarism. The savage cannot be reasoned with; barbarous ignorance and heathenish depravity can only be kept in subjection by physical force. We have seen this savagism gradually melt away before the refulgent light of Christianity; we have seen the descendants of these heathens, in multitudes, gathered into our churches; and we have seen the whole institution gradually changing its character – and, as the elevating effect of the Christian religion, it is becoming more and more a patriarchal relation. The bond of union between master and servant is becoming stronger; the master everywhere throughout the South shows more attachment to the family servants; and they, in their turn, show increasing interest in the welfare of the master and his family, and pride themselves more and more in the relation which they sustain. The master everywhere shows a more abiding interest in the true well-being of his servants; the servants exhibit a more trustful confidence in their master as their friend and protector. And so they go to the house of God together, learn their lessons of duty from the same Bible, rejoice in the hopes of a common salvation, and gather together around the table of the same Saviour.

Another manifest effect of religion is seen in the fact that the Negroes are more easily governed where the Gospel exerts its influence on them. We know this is often denied; but the denial is almost always based upon some isolated fact, foreign from the general experience on the subject. Certainly Gospel privileges sometimes harden White men; and it is not unreasonable to expect that the same results may ensue occasionally in the case of ignorant Black men. But this does not prove the general effect to be such. A mere contrast of the character of our servants in this respect, with what they were forty years ago, proves this – for we must not forget that the only elevating influence allowed to operate on them is that of Christianity; for by law they are cut off from all other means of instruction and moral culture. And here it is proper to say, that we are not to expect the influence of Christianity on them to be such as we see it to be on White men. We must remember our superior privileges, our greater capacity, and the eminent advancement of our race; and, at the same time, we must not forget that they are just emerging from heathenish ignorance and savage degradation. The contrast between our own enlightenment and their degradation is immense; and we must expect to see the effects of the Gospel in them to be different in a like degree. We must not judge of their Christian characters too harshly, but must exercise the same charity in judging of them which our missionaries are compelled to do in reference to converts from Paganism.

In the Christian elevation of our servants, in a great degree, lies the safety of the South. We are surrounded by enemies, who would teach them to look upon you as their worst oppressors and their direst foes – who would array against you their most virulent passions and their bitterest hate. But by the inculcation of Christian principles, sanctified of God, these passions are checked, and this hatred assuaged; and they learn to know and understand the nature of mutual obligations and reciprocal interests; they begin to ascertain that their best friends are those who care for them and do for them as to the interests of time, and who are concerned, indeed, for their eternal salvation.

How beautifully does all duty harmonize with all human welfare and advantage. We have thus spoken to you as to your duty. Let us say a word as to your interest. It is not worth the while to argue with you the question of the relative advantage which that man has whose servants are trained to honesty and a conscientious discharge of their duties, over one whose servants are vicious and do not obey the dictates of conscience and religion. This shows itself in the very market – but more still on the plantation, in the devotion of the servants to the interests of their master, and to the welfare of the master's family. This will be in precise proportion to the degree of interest the master shows in protecting their moral rights and securing their personal comfort, and opportunities of religious worship. This view of the subject, however, is the lowest possible, and we would fondly hope, brethren beloved, that those higher motives already mentioned will have a more binding force on your consciences. As to the best methods of instruction, we desire to say a few words. The three leading systems employed among us, are those of public preaching at the church, plantation preaching, and oral instruction. These different methods are all good, and ought to be employed – all of them – wherever practicable; as they are capable of being used in conjunction, and also separately. The pastors and ministers of this Presbytery, wherever circumstances render it important, are now in the habit of holding public services, especially designed for servants, which we highly approve, and exhort its continuance. Arrangements are made by others for plantation preaching in the bounds of their respective charges to a greater or less extent. But it is manifest that no man can discharge all the duties pertaining to this subject, in connection with regular pastoral labor in White congregations, if large; and even where this is practicable, the religious care of the servants, on the part of the master, does not end with it. We would recommend you all most earnestly to establish on your plantations regular Sabbath instruction in the catechism prepared for the oral instruction of servants, by the Rev. Dr. C.C. Jones, of Georgia, in connection with efforts to inculcate knowledge by the committing of hymns, portions of Scripture, etc., in the same way; which may well be done by masters themselves, or by laymen employed as catechists. But, after all, the great matter is to have the duty well and faithfully done, and that regularly and constantly. The manner is important; but must be determined much by circumstances. To you, in the fear of the Lord, we commit the matter, trusting that, by the Divine blessing, and with the counsel and help of your ministers and church sessions, you may be enabled with fidelity to discharge these great and important duties.

And here let us remind you, that the same Gospel by which we hope to be saved, is the Gospel by which our servants are to be saved. We are Presbyterians, rejoicing in the doctrines of grace taught in the Bible and embodied in our standards. If they are the truth of God, as we believe, how dare we refuse to teach them to our servants? And yet, how many are there among us, who think that these doctrines are unsuitable for the lowly and the ignorant, and who refuse to make provision for the instruction of their servants in those very truths which they themselves believe! It is well to allow servants the right, as is common among us, of enjoying such religious worship as they conscientiously prefer; but when you, as masters, undertake to secure religious instruction for them, if possible, let it be in that form which accords the most nearly with what you conscientiously believe to be contained in the Bible. But here we do not wish to leave room for any misunderstanding. We would by no means discourage you in providing for the religions instruction of your servants where preaching of our own order may not be attainable. While we would urge you to secure them Gospel privileges equal to your own, if possible, at the same time, if ministers of our own Church cannot be obtained, we would exhort you, by all means, to secure preaching for them from any of the various denominations which we recognize as holding the evangelical doctrines of the Gospel; and thus secure for them the best privileges in your power. But, brethren, in addition to these public and special means of instruction, there are personal duties which you alone can discharge, individually, to your own servants; some of which we shall briefly mention.

1. Train your servants to remember to keep holy the Sabbath. We believe we know of no instance in which any direct or flagrant violation of that sacred day has been required or authorized by any of our people. But we think the common custom of requiring servants to appear in clean dress on Monday morning to be of pernicious tendency. You give them time on Saturday to make their preparations for the Sabbath, which they often squander in idleness, and then make up the lost time secretly on the Sabbath. Were they required to present themselves in clean dress on Sabbath morning, it would remove this temptation to violate the Sabbath; and, besides, would make the

difficulty infinitely less of persuading them to go to church, and to attend on catechetical instruction, and other ordinances or services of religion.

2. Train them to go to church from their childhood. Were we to be remiss in training our children to go to church until they were grown, we would find but little disposition in them to go when they had arrived at years of maturity. So with our servants. Train them to regular attendance on the ordinances from their childhood, and when grown up, you will find but little difficulty in securing their attendance on church.

3. Be careful to protect them in the enjoyment of the rights, and encourage them in the discharge of the duties of the family. The chiefest of these rights is that of marriage. Unfortunately the law does not throw its protection around them in this behalf; although public sentiment, which is nearly as powerful as law, does. But yet, sometimes by removals and deaths, occasions of hardship under this head occur, although we hope not among you. But yet, so sacred are these rights to your servants, and so debasing must be any denial of them, that we feel it our duty to put you on your guard, and renewedly to invoke your diligence, exhorting you rather to suffer pecuniary damage yourselves, than to allow moral wrong to accrue to your servants. Did they know that they were absolutely protected from wrong in the wanton dissevering of the tie of marriage, they would value it more, and cherish it with more constancy.

Again, encourage them in the discharge of proper parental duties towards their children, especially whenever they seem to estimate their responsibilities aright, and aim to discharge them on Christian principles. Encourage them, also, where the parents are pious, to hold domestic worship; which is itself one of the primary Christian duties; but, besides, it is one of the surest means of confirming the family tie, and one of the divinely associated means of training children to the practice of righteousness and the knowledge of salvation. And, then, not only grant them the right, but urge them to embrace the privilege of presenting their children for Christian baptism. By these means much may be done to rescue the family tie from neglect, to make them value its privileges and enjoy its blessings.

4. Be careful to set before your servants a godly example. Let them see in your lives the truth and power of the Christian religion; and thus you may lead them to admire, and, by God's blessing, to choose the ways of holiness.

5. In like manner, while you set them such an example yourselves, do not suffer any one to exercise authority over them in your name who will set them a contrary example. Do not suffer them to hear profanity, nor to be sworn at, or cursed by any one placed in authority over them by you. It is debasing to them, as human beings, to be thus addressed in administering reproof or giving commands; but, besides, it sets them an example of evil which too often takes root in their hearts, and matures itself in their lives. Let it not, therefore, be heard of on the plantations of Christian masters.

6. So, also, let us charge you to look carefully into the character of the servants you add to your households. The efforts and labors of many years for the moral elevation of your servants may all come to naught by your introducing to their daily and necessary companionship persons of de-

praved dispositions and vicious lives. "Evil communications corrupt good manners."

7. Pray with your servants and pray for them. Teach your servants to know and feel that you care for them – that you desire their temporal welfare – that you vindicate their moral rights – and that you are deeply concerned for their salvation; and you will not only have won their hearts afresh, but you will thereby have done much to lead them to consider the great question of their salvation. And, then, God is a hearer and answerer of prayer, and by faithful effort on our part, and with constant prayer to God, we may expect to secure the Divine favor in the salvation of our servants, as of our families.

Finally, brethren, remember, "that ye also have a Master in heaven." For all the deeds done in the body we must give account unto God; and especially is this so of you masters, to whom He has committed this great stewardship, involving the personal care, the civil protection, the moral elevation, the religious training, and the final salvation of your servants. These duties devolve on you, not only by the laws of the State, which commits them to you so absolutely that nothing can be done nor attempted without your co-operation; but, also, by the law of Christ, which exhorts you to give the Gospel to every creature, – commands you to render unto your servants that which is just and equal, – declares "that whatsoever good thing any man doeth, the same shall he receive of the Lord, whether bond or free," and hence only promises its blessings on you, when you train, not only your children, but your households to the service of God. For your fidelity in the discharge of this stewardship, the Great Master Himself will call you to a reckoning – that same Master, Jesus, who died for you, and who died for them. And, know assuredly, that whosoever giveth a cup of cold water to a disciple, even the humblest, in the name of a disciple, shall receive a disciple's reward. Remember at all times, and in the discharge of all duties, the judgment seat to which both you and your servants are rapidly hurrying, and strive so to live and act as to receive yourselves, and secure for them, the glad welcome of good and faithful servants. Strive to be so faithful to your servants, in this behalf, that, by God's blessing, you may render their lives upright and Christian – that you may animate them in the midst of their toil for you with the hopes of an immortality of blessedness – and that at death they may close their eyes in the sweet sleep of the Christian, invoking and pronouncing on your heads the blessings of grateful hearts, as they pass from you to the uninterrupted service of the Master above, there to await you, and to become stars in your crown of rejoicing, when you also shall be called up. And, oh! brethren, be so faithful, that at that day and hour of fearful reckoning, it shall not be brought to your charge, that your want of faithfulness has consigned any of your servants to the doom of a fearful hell.

Brethren beloved in the Lord, we are done. With all simplicity and fidelity we have aimed to lay before you your whole duty in this great and responsible matter, not doubting that what we have said will meet a unanimous response from all of your hearts, and we trust will produce its fruit in your lives. If you can justify yourselves, happy are you, and God shall bless you. If you are constrained to confess much shortcoming – as, alas! we know many must

– then, brethren, let us trust that, by God's grace, you will now begin to discharge your duty. And let us all remember that our time is short, and whatever we do must be done quickly. May we all, ministers and people, masters and servants, so live and so act, that when we shall be called hence we shall meet together in the great congregation above.

And may the grace of the Lord Jesus Christ be with you all. Amen.

❧

E. T. Baird was the pastor of the Presbyterian Church in Crawfordsville, Mississippi. He served as Acting Stated Clerk of the Second General Assembly of the Presbyterian Church in the Confederate States of America in 1862.

This article was originally prepared as a Pastoral Letter of the Tombeckbee Presbytery to the churches and people under its care. It appeared in the *Southern Presbyterian Review*, July 1859, Vol. XII, No. 2.

V

The South, Her Peril and Her Duty
by Rev. Benjamin Morgan Palmer, D.D.

Psalm 94:20. Shall the throne of iniquity have fellowship with thee, which frameth mischief by a law?

Obadiah 7. All the men of thy confederacy have brought thee even to the border: the men that were at peace with thee have deceived thee, and prevailed against thee; they that eat thy bread have laid a wound under thee: there is none understanding in him.

The voice of the Chief Magistrate has summoned us today to the house of prayer. This call, in its annual repetition, may be too often only a solemn State-form; nevertheless it covers a mighty and a double truth.

It recognizes the existence of a personal God whose will shapes the destiny of nations, and that sentiment of religion in man which points to Him as the needle to the pole. Even with those who grope in the twilight of natural religion, natural conscience gives a voice to the dispensations of Providence. If in autumn "extensive harvests hang their heavy head," the joyous reaper, "crowned with the sickle and the wheaten sheaf," lifts his heart to the "Father of Lights from whom cometh down every good and perfect gift." Or, if pestilence and famine waste the earth, even pagan altars smoke with bleeding victims, and costly hecatombs appease the divine anger which flames out in such dire misfortunes. It is the instinct of man's religious nature, which, among Christians and heathen alike, seeks after God – the natural homage which reason, blinded as it may be, pays to a universal and ruling Providence. All classes bow beneath its spell especially in seasons of gloom, when a nation bends beneath the weight of a general calamity, and a common sorrow falls upon every heart. The hesitating skeptic forgets to weigh his scruples, as the dark shadow passes over him and fills his soul with awe. The dainty philosopher, coolly discoursing of the forces of nature and her uniform laws, abandons, for a time, his atheistical speculations, abashed by the proofs of a supreme and personal will.

Thus the devout followers of Jesus Christ, and those who do not rise above the level of mere theism, are drawn into momentary fellowship; as under the pressure of these inextinguishable convictions they pay a public and united homage to the God of nature and of grace.

In obedience to this great law of religious feeling, not less than in obedience to the civil ruler who represents this commonwealth in its unity, we are now assembled. Hitherto, on similar occasions, our language has been the language of gratitude and song. "The voice of rejoicing and salvation was in the tabernacles of the righteous." Together we praised the Lord "that our garners were full, affording all manner of store; that our sheep brought forth thousands and ten thousands in our streets; that our oxen were strong to labor, and there was no breaking in nor going out, and no complaining was in our streets." As we together surveyed the blessings of Providence, the joyful chorus swelled from millions of people, "Peace be within thy walls and prosperity within thy palaces." But, to-day, burdened hearts all over this land are brought to the sanctuary of God. We "see the tents of Cushan in affliction, and the curtains of the land of Midian do tremble." We have fallen upon times when there are "signs in the sun, and in the moon, and in the stars; upon the earth distress of nations, with perplexity; the sea and the waves roaring; men's hearts failing them for fear and for looking after those things which are coming" in the near yet gloomy future. Since the words of this proclamation were penned by which we are convened, that which all men dreaded, but against which all men hoped, has been realized; and in the triumph of a sectional majority we are compelled to read the probable doom of our once happy and united confederacy. It is not to be concealed that we are in the most fearful and perilous crisis which has occurred in our history as a nation. The cords which, during four-fifths of a century, have bound together this growing republic are now strained to their utmost tension: they just need the touch of fire to part asunder forever. Like a ship laboring in the storm and suddenly grounded upon some treacherous shoal – every timber of this vast confederacy strains and groans under the pressure. Sectional divisions, the jealousy of rival interests, the lust of political power, a bastard ambition which looks to personal aggrandizement rather than to the public weal, a reckless radicalism which seeks for the subversion of all that is ancient and stable, and a furious fanaticism which drives on its ill-considered conclusions with utter disregard of the evil it engenders – all these combine to create a portentous crisis, the like of which we have never known before, and which puts to a crucifying test the virtue, the patriotism and the piety of the country. You, my hearers, who have waited upon my public ministry and have known me in the intimacies of pastoral intercourse, will do me the justice to testify that I have never intermeddled with political questions. Interested as I might be in the progress of events, I have never obtruded, either publicly or privately, my opinions upon any of you; nor can a single man arise and say that, by word or sign, have I ever sought to warp his sentiments or control his judgment upon any political subject whatsoever. The party questions which have hitherto divided the political world, have seemed to me to involve no issue sufficiently momentous to warrant my turning aside, even for a moment, from my chosen calling. In this day of intelligence, I have felt there were thousands around me more competent to instruct in statesmanship; and thus, from considerations of modesty no less than prudence, I have preferred to move among you as a preacher of righteousness belonging to a Kingdom not of this world.

During the heated canvass which has just been brought to so disastrous a close, the seal of a rigid and religious silence has not been broken. I deplored the divisions amongst us as being, to a large extent, impertinent in the solemn crisis which was too evidently impending. Most clearly did it appear to me that but one issue was before us; an issue soon to be presented in a form which would compel the attention. That crisis might make it imperative upon me as a Christian and a divine to speak in language admitting no misconstruction. Until then, aside from the din and strife of parties, I could only mature, with solitary and prayerful thought, the destined utterance. That hour has come. At a juncture so solemn as the present, with the destiny of a great people waiting upon the decision of an hour, it is not lawful to be still. Whoever may have influence to shape public opinion, at such a time must lend it, or prove faithless to a trust as solemn as any to be accounted for at the bar of God.

Is it immodest in me to assume that I may represent a class whose opinions in such a controversy are of cardinal importance? The class which seeks to ascertain its duty in the light simply of conscience and religion; and which turns to the moralist and the Christian for support and guidance. The question, too, which now places us upon the brink of revolution, was in its origin a question of morals and religion. It was debated in ecclesiastical councils before it entered legislative halls. It has riven asunder the two largest religious communions in the land: and the right determination of this primary question will go far toward fixing the attitude we must assume in the coming struggle. I sincerely pray God that I may be forgiven if I have misapprehended the duty incumbent upon me to-day; for I have ascended this pulpit under the agitation of feeling natural to one who is about to deviate from the settled policy of his public life. It is my purpose – not as your organ, compromitting you, whose opinions are for the most part unknown to me, but on my sole responsibility – to speak upon the one question of the day; and to state the

duty which, as I believe, patriotism and religion alike require of us all. I shall aim to speak with a moderation of
tone and feeling almost judicial, well befitting the sanctities
of the place and the solemnities of the judgment day.

In determining our duty in this emergency it is necessary that we should first ascertain the nature of the trust
providentially committed to us. A nation often has a
character as well defined and intense as that of the individual. This depends, of course upon a variety of causes
operating through a long period of time. It is due largely to
the original traits which distinguish the stock from which
it springs, and to the providential training which has
formed its education. But, however derived, this individu-
ality of character alone makes any people truly historic,
competent to work out its specific mission, and to become
a factor in the world's progress. The particular trust
assigned to such a people becomes the pledge of the divine
protection; and their fidelity to it determines the fate by
which it is finally overtaken. What that trust is must be
ascertained from the necessities of their position, the
institutions which are the outgrowth of their principles and
the conflicts through which they preserve their identity and
independence.

If then the South is such a people, what, at this juncture, is their providential trust? I answer, that it is *to conserve and to perpetuate the institution of domestic slavery as
now existing*. It is not necessary here to inquire whether this
is precisely the best relation in which the hewer of wood
and drawer of water can stand to his employer; although
this proposition may perhaps be successfully sustained by
those who choose to defend it. Still less are we required,

dogmatically, to affirm that it will subsist through all time. Baffled as our wisdom may now be, in finding a solution of this intricate social problem, it would nevertheless be the height of arrogance to pronounce what changes may or may not occur in the distant future. In the grand march of events Providence may work out a solution undiscoverable by us. What modifications of soil and climate may hereafter be produced, what consequent changes in the products on which we depend, what political revolutions may occur among the races which are now enacting the great drama of history: all such inquiries are totally irrelevant because no prophetic vision can pierce the darkness of that future. If this question should ever arise, the generation to whom it is remitted will doubtless have the wisdom to meet it, and Providence will furnish the lights in which it is to be resolved. All that we claim for them and for ourselves is liberty to work out this problem guided by nature and God, without obtrusive interference from abroad. These great questions of Providence and history must have free scope for their solution; and the race whose fortunes are distinctly implicated in the same is alone authorized, as it is alone competent, to determine them.

It is just this impertinence of human legislation, setting bounds to what God only can regulate, that the South is called this day to resent and resist. The country is convulsed simply because "the throne of iniquity frameth mischief by a law." Without, therefore, determining the question of duty for future generations, I simply say, that for us, as now situated, the duty is plain of conserving and transmitting the system of slavery, with the freest scope for its natural development and extension. Let us, my brethren, look our duty in the face. With this institution assigned to our keeping, what reply shall we make to those who say that its days are numbered? My own conviction is, that we should at once lift ourselves, intelligently, to the highest moral ground and proclaim to all the world that we hold this trust from God, and in its occupancy we are prepared to stand or fall as God may appoint. If the critical moment has arrived at which the great issue is joined, let us say that, in the sight of all perils, we will stand by our trust; and God be with the right!

The argument which enforces the solemnity of this providential trust is simple and condensed. It is bound upon us, then, by the *principle of self-preservation,* that "first law" which is continually asserting its supremacy over all others. Need I pause to show how this system of servitude underlies and supports our material interests? That our wealth consists in our lands and in the serfs who till them? That from the nature of our products they can only be culti-vated by labor which must be controlled in order to be certain? That any other than a tropical race must faint and wither beneath a tropical sun? Need I pause to show how this system is interwoven with our entire social fabric? That these slaves form parts of our households, even as our children; and that, too, through a relationship recognized and sanctioned in the Scriptures of God even as the other? Must I pause to show how it has fashioned our modes of life, and determined all our habits of thought and feeling, and molded the very type of our civilization? How then can the hand of violence be laid upon it without involving our existence? The so-called free States of this country are working out the social problem under conditions peculiar to themselves. These conditions are sufficiently hard, and their success is too uncertain, to excite in us the least jealousy of their lot. With a teeming population, which the soil cannot support – with their wealth depending upon arts, created by artificial wants – with an eternal friction between the grades of their society – with their labor and their capital grinding against each other like the upper and nether millstones – with labor cheapened and displaced by new mechanical inventions, bursting more asunder the bonds of brotherhood; amid these intricate perils we have ever given them our sympathy and our prayers, and have never sought to weaken the foundations of their social order. God grant them complete success in the solution of all their perplexities! We, too, have our responsibilities and trials; but they are all bound up in this one institution, which has been the object of such unrighteous assault through five and twenty years. If we are true to ourselves we shall, at this critical juncture, stand by it and work out our destiny.

This duty is bound upon us again *as the constituted guardians of the slaves themselves.* Our lot is not more implicated in theirs, than is their lot in ours; in our mutual relations we survive or perish together. The worst foes of the Black race are those who have intermeddled on their behalf. We know better than others that every attribute of their character fits them for dependence and servitude. By nature the most affectionate and loyal of all races beneath the sun, they are also the most helpless: and no calamity can befall them greater than the loss of that protection they enjoy under this patriarchal system. Indeed the experiment has been grandly tried of precipitating them upon freedom which they know not how to enjoy; and the dismal results are before us in statistics that astonish the world. With the fairest portions of the earth in their possession and with the advantage of a long discipline as cultivators of the soil, their constitutional indolence has converted the most beautiful islands of the sea into a howling waste. It is not too much to say that if the South should, at this moment, surrender every slave, the wisdom of the entire world, united in solemn council, could not solve the question of their disposal. Their transportation to Africa, even if it were feasible, would be but the most refined cruelty; they must perish with starvation before they could have time to relapse into their primitive barbarism. Their residence here, in the presence of the vigorous Saxon race, would be but the signal for their rapid extermination before they had time to waste away through listlessness, filth, and vice. Freedom would be their doom; and equally from both they call upon us, their providential guardians, to be protected. I know this argument will be scoffed abroad as the hypocritical cover thrown over our own cupidity and selfishness; but every Southern master knows its truth and feels its power. My servant, whether born in my house or bought with my money, stands to me in the relation of a child. Though providentially owing me service, which, providentially, I am bound to exact, he is, nevertheless, my brother and my friend; and I am to him a guardian and a father. He leans upon me for protection, for counsel, and for blessing; and so long as the relation continues, no power, but the power of almighty God, shall come between him and me. Were there no argument but this, it binds upon us the providential duty of preserving the relation that we may save him from a doom worse than death.

It is a duty which we owe, further, *to the civilized world*. It is a remarkable fact that during these thirty years of unceasing warfare against slavery, and while a lying spirit has inflamed the world against us, that world has grown more and more dependent upon it for sustenance and wealth. Every tyro knows that all branches of industry fall back upon the soil. We must come, every one of us, to the bosom of this great mother for nourishment. In the happy partnership which has grown up in providence between the tribes of this confederacy, our industry has been concentrated upon agriculture. To the North we have cheerfully resigned all the profits arising from manufacture and commerce. Those profits they have, for the most part, fairly earned, and we have never begrudged them. We have sent them our sugar and bought it back when refined; we have sent them our cotton and bought it back when spun into thread or woven into cloth. Almost every article we use, from the shoe lachet to the most elaborate and costly article of luxury, they have made and we have bought; and both sections have thriven by the partnership, as no people ever thrived before since the first shining of the sun. So literally true are the words of the text, addressed by Obadiah to Edom, "All the men of our confederacy, the men that were at peace with us, have eaten our bread at the very time they have deceived and laid a wound under us." Even beyond, this the enriching commerce, which has built the splendid cities and marble palaces, of England as well as of America, has been largely established upon the products of our soil; and the blooms upon Southern fields gathered by Black hands, have fed the spindles and looms of Manchester and Birmingham not less than of Lawrence and Lowell. Strike now a blow at this system of labor and the world itself totters at the stroke. Shall we permit that blow to fall? Do we not owe it to civilized man to stand in the breach and stay the uplifted arm? If the blind Samson lays hold of the pillars which support the arch of the world's industry, how many more will be buried beneath its ruins than the lords of the Philistines? "Who knoweth whether we are not come to the kingdom for such a time as this."

Last of all, in this great struggle, *we defend the cause of God and religion.* The Abolition spirit is undeniably atheistic. The demon which erected its throne upon the guillotine in the days of Robespierre and Marat, which abolished the Sabbath and worshiped reason in the person of a harlot, yet survives to work other horrors, of which those of the French revolution are but the type. Among a people so generally religious as the American, a disguise must be worn; but it is the same old threadbare disguise of the advocacy of human rights. From a thousand Jacobin clubs here, as in France, the decree has gone forth which strikes at God by striking at all subordination and law. Availing itself of the morbid and misdirected sympathies of men, it has entrapped weak consciences in the meshes of its treachery; and now, at last, has seated its high priest upon the throne, clad in the black garments of discord and schism, so symbolic of its ends. Under this specious cry of reform, it demands that every evil shall be corrected, or society become a wreck – the sun must be stricken from the heavens, if a spot is found upon his disc. The Most High, knowing His own power which is infinite, and His own wisdom which is unfathomable, can afford to be patient. But these self-constituted reformers must quicken the activity of Jehovah or compel His abdication. In their furious haste, they trample upon obligations sacred as any which can bind the conscience.

It is time to reproduce the obsolete idea that Providence must govern man, and not that man should control Providence. In the imperfect state of human society, it pleases God to allow evils which check others that are greater. As in the physical world, objects are moved forward, not by a single force, but by the composition of forces; so in His moral administration, there are checks and balances whose intimate relations are comprehended only by Himself. But what reck they of this – these fierce zealots who undertake to drive the chariot of the sun? Working out the single and false idea which rides them like a nightmare, they dash athwart the spheres, utterly disregarding the delicate mechanism of Providence; which moves on, wheels within wheels, with pivots and balances and springs, which the great Designer alone can control. This spirit of atheism, which knows no God who tolerates evil, no Bible which sanctions law, and no conscience that can be bound by oaths and covenants, has selected us for its victims, and slavery for its issue. Its banner-cry rings out already upon the air –"liberty, equality, fraternity," which simply interpreted mean bondage, confiscation and massacre. With its tricolor waving in the breeze, it waits to inaugurate its reign of terror.

To the South the high position is assigned of defending, before all nations, the cause of all religion and of all truth. In this trust, we are resisting the power which wars against constitutions and laws and compacts, against Sabbaths and sanctuaries, against the Family, the State, and the Church; which blasphemously invades the prerogatives of God, and rebukes the Most High for the errors of His administration; which, if it cannot snatch the reins of empire from His grasp, will lay the universe in ruins at His feet. Is it possible that we shall decline the onset?

This argument, then, which sweeps over the entire circle of our relations, touches the four cardinal points of duty *to ourselves, to our slaves, to the world, and to Almighty God*. It establishes the nature and solemnity of our present trust, *to preserve and transmit our existing system of domestic servitude, with the right, unchallenged by man, to go and root itself wherever Providence and nature may carry it*. This trust we will discharge in the face of the worst possible peril. Though war be the aggregation of all evils, yet, should the madness of the hour appeal to the arbitration of the sword, we will not shrink even from the baptism of fire. If modern crusaders stand in serried ranks upon some plain of Esdraelon, there shall we be in defense of our trust. Not till the last man has fallen behind the last rampart, shall it drop from our hands; and then only in surrender to the God who gave it.

Against this institution a system of aggression has been pursued through the last thirty years. Initiated by a few fanatics, who were at first despised, it has gathered strength from opposition until it has assumed its present gigantic proportions. No man has thoughtfully watched the progress of this controversy without being convinced that the crisis must at length come. Some few, perhaps, have hoped against hope, that the gathering imposthume might be dispersed, and the poison be eliminated from the body politic by healthful remedies. But the delusion has scarcely been cherished by those who have studied the history of fanaticism in its path of blood and fire through the ages of the past. The moment must arrive when the conflict must be joined, and victory decide for one or the other. As it has been a war of legislative tactics, and not of physical force, both parties have been maneuvering for a position; and the embarrassment has been, whilst dodging amidst constitutional forms, to make an issue that should be clear, simple, and tangible. Such an issue is at length presented in the result of the recent Presidential election. Be it observed, too, that it is an issue made by the North, not by the South; upon whom, therefore, must rest the entire guilt of the present disturbance. With a choice between three national candidates, who have more or less divided the votes of the South, the North, with unexampled unanimity, have cast their ballot for a candidate who is sectional, who represents a party that is sectional, and the ground of that sectionalism, prejudice against the established and constitutional rights and immunities and institutions of the South. What does this declare – what can it declare, but that from henceforth this is to be a government of section over section; a government using constitutional forms only to embarrass and divide the section ruled, and as fortresses through whose embrasures the cannon of legislation is to be employed in demolishing the guaranteed institutions of the South? What issue is more direct, concrete, intelligible than this? I thank God that, since the conflict must be joined, the responsibility of this issue rests not with us, who have ever acted upon the defensive; and that it is so disembarrassed and simple that the feeblest mind can understand it.

The question with the South to-day is not what issue shall she make, but how shall she meet that which is prepared for her? Is it possible that we can hesitate longer than a moment? In our natural recoil from the perils of revolution, and with our clinging fondness for the memories of the past, we may perhaps look around for something to soften the asperity of this issue, for some ground on which we may defer the day of evil, for some hope that the gathering clouds may not burst in fury upon the land.

It is alleged, for example, that the President elect has been chosen by a fair majority under prescribed forms. But need I say, to those who have read history, that no despotism is more absolute than that of an unprincipled democracy, and no tyranny more galling than that exercised through constitutional formulas? But the plea is idle, when the very question we debate is the perpetuation of that Constitution now converted into an engine of oppression, and the continuance of that Union which is henceforth to be our condition of vassalage. I say it with solemnity and pain, this Union of our forefathers is already gone. It existed but in mutual confidence, the bonds of which were ruptured in the late election. Though its form should be preserved, it is, in fact, destroyed. We may possibly entertain the project of reconstructing it; but it will be another union, resting upon other than past guarantees. "In that we say a new covenant we have made the first old, and that which decayeth and waxeth old is ready to vanish away" – "as a vesture it is folded up." For myself I say that, under the rule which threatens us, I throw off the yoke of this

Union as readily as did our ancestors the yoke of King George III, and for causes immeasurably stronger than those pleaded in their celebrated declaration.

It is softly whispered, too, that the successful competitor for the throne protests and avers his purpose to administer the government in a conservative and national spirit. Allowing him all credit for personal integrity in these protestations, he is, in this matter, nearly as impotent for good as he is competent for evil. He is nothing more than a figure upon the political chess-board – whether pawn or knight or king, will hereafter appear – but still a silent figure upon the checkered squares, moved by the hands of an unseen player. That player is the party to which he owes his elevation; a party that has signalized its history by the most unblushing perjuries. What faith can be placed in the protestations of men who openly avow that their consciences are too sublimated to be restrained by the obligation of covenants or by the sanctity of oaths? No; we have seen the trail of the serpent five and twenty years in our Eden; twined now in the branches of the forbidden tree, we feel the pangs of death already begun as its hot breath is upon our cheek, hissing out the original falsehood, "Ye shall not surely die."

Another suggests that even yet the Electors, alarmed by these demonstrations of the South, may not cast the black ball which dooms their country to the executioner. It is a forlorn hope. Whether we should counsel such breach of faith in them or take refuge in their treachery – whether such a result would give a President chosen by the people according to the Constitution – are points I will not discuss. But that it would prove a cure for any of our ills, who can believe! It is certain that it would, with some show of justice, exasperate a party sufficiently ferocious; that it would doom us to four years of increasing strife and bitterness; and that the crisis must come at last under issues possibly not half so clear as the present. Let us not desire to shift the day of trial by miserable subterfuges of this sort. The issue is upon us; let us meet it like men and end this strife forever.

But some quietist whispers, yet further, this majority is accidental and has been swelled by accessions of men simply opposed to the existing administration; the party is utterly heterogeneous and must be shivered into fragments by its own success. I confess, frankly, this suggestion has staggered me more than any other, and I sought to take refuge therein. Why should we not wait and see the effect of success itself upon a party whose elements might devour each other in the very distribution of the spoil? Two considerations have dissipated the fallacy before me. The first is, that, however mixed the party, Abolitionism is clearly its informing and actuating soul; and fanaticism is a blood-hound that never bolts its track when it has once lapped blood. The elevation of their candidate is far from being the consummation of their aims. It is only the beginning of that consummation; and, if all history be not a lie, there will be cohesion enough till the end of the beginning is reached, and the dreadful banquet of slaughter and ruin shall glut the appetite.

The second consideration is a principle which I cannot blink. It is nowhere denied that the first article in the creed of the now dominant party is the restriction of slavery within its present limits. It is distinctly avowed by their organs, and in the name of their elected chieftain; as will appear from the following extract from an article written to pacify the South and to reassure its fears:

There can be no doubt whatever in the mind of any man, that Mr. Lincoln regards slavery as a moral, social, and political evil, and that it should be dealt with as such by the Federal Government, in every instance where it is called upon to deal with it at all. On this point there is no room for question, and there need be no misgivings as to his official action. The whole influence of the Executive Department of the Government, while in his hands, will be thrown against the extension of slavery into the new territories of the Union, and the re-opening of the African slave trade. On these points he will make no compromise nor yield one hair's breadth to coercion from any quarter or in any shape. He does not accede to the alleged decision of the Supreme Court, that the Constitution places slaves upon the footing of other property, and protects them as such wherever its jurisdiction extends, nor will he be, in the least degree, governed or controlled by it in his executive action. He will do all in his power, personally and officially, by the direct exercise of the powers of his office, and the indirect influence inseparable from it, to arrest the tendency to make slavery national and perpetual, and to place it in precisely the same position which it held in the early days of the Republic, and in the view of the founders of the Government.

Now, what enigmas may be couched in this last sentence, the sphinx which uttered them can perhaps resolve; but the sentence in which they occur is as big as the belly of the Trojan horse which laid the city of Priam in ruins.

These utterances we have heard so long that they fall stale upon the ear; but never before have they had such significance. Hitherto they have come from Jacobin conventicles and pulpits, from the rostrum, from the hustings, and from the halls of our national Congress: but always as the utterances of irresponsible men or associations of men. But now the voice comes from the throne; already, before clad with the sanctities of office, ere the anointing oil is poured upon the monarch's head, the decree has gone forth that the institution of Southern slavery shall be constrained within assigned limits. Though nature and Providence should send forth its branches like the Banyan tree, to take root in congenial soil, here is a power superior to both, that says it shall wither and die within its own charmed circle.

What say you to this, to whom this great providential trust of conserving slavery is assigned? "Shall the throne of iniquity have fellowship with thee, which frameth mischief by a law?" It is this that makes the crisis. Whether we will or not, this is the historic moment when the fate of this institution hangs suspended in the balance. Decide either way, it is the moment of our destiny – the only thing affected by the decision is the complexion of that destiny. If the South bows before this throne, she accepts the decree of restriction and ultimate extinction, which is made the condition of her homage.

As it appears to me, the course to be pursued in this emergency is that which has already been inaugurated. Let the people in all the Southern States, in solemn council assembled, reclaim the powers they have delegated. Let those conventions be composed of men whose fidelity has been approved – men who bring the wisdom, experience and firmness of age to support and announce principles which have long been matured. Let these conventions decide firmly and solemnly what they will do with this great trust committed to their hands. Let them pledge each other in sacred covenant, to uphold and perpetuate what they cannot resign without dishonor and palpable ruin. Let them further, take all the necessary steps looking to separate and independent existence; and initiate measures for framing a new and homogeneous confederacy. Thus, prepared for every contingency, let the crisis come. Paradoxical as it may seem, if there be any way to save, or rather to re-construct, the Union of our forefathers, it is this. Perhaps, at the last moment, the conservative portions of the North may awake to see the abyss into which they are about to plunge. Perchance they may arise and crush out forever the Abolition hydra, and cast it into a grave from which there shall never be a resurrection.

Thus, with restored confidence, we may be rejoined a united and happy people. But, before God, I believe that nothing will effect this but the line of policy which the South has been compelled in self-preservation to adopt. I confess frankly, I am not sanguine that such an auspicious result will be reached. Partly, because I do not see how new guarantees are to be grafted upon the Constitution, nor how, if grafted, they can be more binding than those which have already been trampled under foot; but chiefly, because I do not see how such guarantees can be elicited from the people at the North. It cannot be disguised, that almost to a man, they are anti-slavery where they are not Abolition. A whole generation has been educated to look upon the system with abhorrence – as a national blot. They hope, and look, and pray for its extinction within a reasonable time, and cannot be satisfied unless things are seen drawing to that conclusion. We, on the contrary, as its constituted guardians, can demand nothing less than that it should be left open to expansion, subject to no limitations save those imposed by God and nature. I fear the antagonism is too great, and the conscience of both parties too deeply implicated to allow such a composition of the strife. Nevertheless since it is within the range of possibility in the Providence of God, I would not shut out the alternative.

Should it fail, what remains but that we say to each other, calmly and kindly, what Abraham said to Lot: "Let there be no strife, I pray thee, between me and thee, and between my herdmen and thy herdmen, for we be brethren: Is not the whole land before thee? Separate thyself, I pray thee, from me; if thou will take the left hand, then I will go to the right, or if thou depart to the right hand, then I will go to the left." Thus, if we cannot save the Union, we may save the inestimable blessings it enshrines; if we cannot preserve the vase, we will preserve the precious liquor it contains.

In all this, I speak for the North no less than for the South; for upon our united and determined resistance at this moment, depends the salvation of the whole country; in saving ourselves we shall save the North from the ruin she is madly drawing down upon her own head.

The position of the South is at this moment sublime. If she has grace given her to know her hour, she will save herself, the country, and the world. It will involve, indeed, temporary prostration and distress; the dykes of Holland must be cut to save her from the troops of Philip. But I warn my countrymen, the historic moment once passed never returns. If she will arise in her majesty, and speak now as with the voice of one man, she will roll back, for all time, the curse that is upon her. If she succumbs now, she transmits that curse as an heirloom to posterity. We may, for a generation, enjoy comparative ease, gather up our feet in our beds, and die in peace; but our children will go forth beggared from the homes of their fathers. Fishermen will cast their nets where your proud commercial navy now rides at anchor, and dry them upon the shore now covered with your bales of merchandise. Sapped, circumvented, undermined, the institutions of your soil will be overthrown; and within five and twenty years, the history of St. Domingo will be the record of Louisiana. If dead men's bones can tremble, ours will move under the muttered curses of sons and daughters, denouncing the blindness and love of ease which have left them an inheritance of woe.

I have done my duty under as deep a sense of responsibility to God and man, as I have ever felt. Under a full conviction that the salvation of the whole country is depending upon the action of the South, I am impelled to deepen the sentiment of resistance in the Southern mind, and to strengthen the current now flowing towards a union of the South in defense of her chartered rights. It is a duty which I shall not be called to repeat, for such awful junctures do not occur twice in a century. Bright and happy days are yet before us; and before another political earthquake shall shake the continent, I hope to be "where the wicked cease from troubling and where the weary are at rest."

It only remains to say, that whatever be the fortunes of the South, I accept them for my own. Born upon her soil, of a father thus born before me – from an ancestry that occupied it while yet it was a part of England's possessions – she is in every sense, my mother. I shall die upon her bosom – she shall know no peril, but it is my peril – no conflict, but it is my conflict – and no abyss of ruin, into which I shall not share her fall. May the Lord God cover her head in this her day of battle!

Rev. Benjamin Morgan Palmer (1818-1902) was an influential Presbyterian minister and orator. Originally from Charleston, South Carolina, he pastored two congregations in Savannah, Georgia and Columbia, South Carolina before taking the pulpit at First Presbyterian Church in New Orleans, Louisiana, where he remained for the remaining forty-six years of his life. He served as the first moderator of the Presbyterian Church in the Confederate States of America.

The preceding sermon was preached in the First Presbyterian Church in New Orleans on November 29, 1860. This sermon was instrumental in Louisiana's secession from the Union and accession to the Confederate States of America.

V

An Address to all the Churches of Jesus Christ Throughout the World
The First General Assembly of the Presbyterian Church in the Confederate States of America

The General Assembly of the Presbyterian Church in the Confederate States of America to all the Churches of Jesus Christ throughout the earth, greeting: Grace, mercy and peace be multiplied upon you!

Dearly Beloved Brethren:

It is probably known to you that the Presbyteries and Synod in the Confederate States, which were formerly in connection with the General Assembly of the Presbyterian Church in the United States of America, have renounced the jurisdiction of that body; and dissolved the ties which bound them ecclesiastically with their brethren of the North. This act of separation left them without any formal union among themselves. But as they were one in faith and order, and still adhered to their old standards, measures were promptly adopted for giving expression to their unity, by the organization of a Supreme Court, upon the

model of the one whose authority they had just relin-
quished. Commissioners, duly appointed, from all the Presbyteries of these Confederate States, met accordingly, in
the city of Augusta, on the fourth day of December, in the
year of our Lord one thousand eight hundred and sixty-
one, and then and there proceeded to constitute the General Assembly of the Presbyterian Church in the Confederate States of America. The Constitution of the Presbyterian
Church in the United States — that is to say, the Westmin-
ster Confession of Faith, the Larger and Shorter Cate-
chisms, the Form of Government, the Book of Discipline,
and the Directory for Worship — were unanimously and
solemnly declared to be the Constitution of the Church in
the Confederate States, with no other change than the sub-
stitution of *Confederate* for *United* wherever the country is
mentioned in the standards. The Church, therefore, in these
seceded States, presents now the spectacle of a separate,
independent and complete organization, under the style
and title of the Presbyterian Church in the Confederate
States of America. In thus taking its place among sister
Churches of this and other countries, it seems proper that
it should set forth the causes which have impelled it to
separate from the Church of the North, and to indicate a
general view of the course which it feels it incumbent upon
it to pursue in the new circumstances in which it is placed.
We should be sorry to be regarded by our brethren in any
part of the world as guilty of schism. We are not conscious
of any purpose to rend the body of Christ. On the contrary,
our aim has been to promote the unity of the Spirit in the
bonds of peace. If we know our own hearts, and can form
any just estimate of the motives which have governed us,

we have been prompted by a sincere desire to promote the glory of God, and the efficiency, energy, harmony and zeal of His visible Kingdom in the earth. We have separated from our brethren of the North as Abraham separated from Lot, because we are persuaded that the interests of true religion will be more effectually subserved by two independent Churches, under the circumstances in which the two countries are placed, than by one united body:

1. In the first place, the course of the last Assembly, at Philadelphia, conclusively shows that if we should remain together, the political questions which divide us as citizens, will be obtruded on our Church Courts, and discussed by Christian Ministers and Elders with all the acrimony, bitterness and rancour with which such questions are usually discussed by men of the world. Our Assembly would present a mournful spectacle of strife and debate. Commissioners from the Northern would meet with Commissioners from the Southern Confederacy, to wrangle over the questions which have split them into two Confederacies, and involved them in furious and bloody war. They would denounce each other, on the one hand, as tyrants and oppressors, and on the other, as traitors and rebels. The Spirit of God would take His departure from these scenes of confusion, and leave the Church lifeless and powerless, an easy prey to the sectional divisions and angry passions of its members. Two nations, under any circumstances, except those of perfect homogeneousness, cannot be united in one Church, without the rigid exclusion of all civil and secular questions from its halls. Where the countries differ in their customs and institutions, and view each other with an eye of jealousy and rivalry, if national feelings are permitted to

enter the Church Courts, there must be an end of harmony and peace. The prejudices of the man and the citizen will prove stronger than the charity of the Christian. When they have allowed themselves to denounce each other for their national peculiarities, it will be hard to join in cordial fellowship as members of the same spiritual family. Much more must this be the case where the nations are not simply rivals, but enemies – when they hate each other with a cruel hatred – when they are engaged in a ferocious and bloody war, and when the worst passions of human nature are stirred to their very depths. An Assembly composed of representatives from two such countries, could have no security for peace except in a steady, uncompromising adherence to the scriptural principle, that it would know no man after the flesh; that it would abolish the distinctions of Barbarian, Scythian, bond and free, and recognize nothing but the new creature in Christ Jesus. The moment it permits itself to know the Confederate or the United States, the moment its members meet as citizens of these countries, our political differences will be transferred to the house of God, and the passions of the forum will expel the Spirit of Holy Love and of Christian communion.

We cannot condemn a man, in one breath, as unfaithful to the most solemn earthly interests, his country and his race, and commend him in the next as a loyal and faithful servant of his God. If we distrust his patriotism, our confidence is apt to be very measured in his piety. The old adage will hold here as in other things, *falsus in uno, falsus in omnibus.*

The only conceivable condition, therefore, upon which the Church of the North and the South could remain together as one body, with any prospect of success, is the rigorous exclusion of the questions and passions of the forum from its halls of debate. This is what always ought to be done. The provinces of Church and State are perfectly distinct, and the one has no right to usurp the jurisdiction of the other. The State is a natural institute, founded in the constitution of man as moral and social, and designed to realize the idea of justice. It is the society of rights. The Church is a supernatural institute, founded in the facts of redemption, and is designed to realize the idea of grace. It is the society of the redeemed. The State aims at social order; the Church at spiritual holiness. The State looks to the visible and outward; the Church is concerned for the invisible and inward. The badge of the State's authority is the sword, by which it becomes a terror to evil doers, and a praise to them that do well. The badge of the Church's authority is the keys, by which it opens and shuts the Kingdom of Heaven, according as men are believing or impenitent. The power of the Church is exclusively spiritual; that of the State includes the exercise of force. The Constitution of the Church is a Divine revelation – the Constitution of the State must be determined by human reason and the course of providential events. The Church has no right to construct or modify a government for the State, and the State has no right to frame a creed or polity for the Church. They are as planets moving in different orbits, and unless each is confined to its own track, the consequences may be as disastrous in the moral world as the collision of different spheres in the world of matter.

It is true that there is a point at which their respective jurisdictions seem to meet – in the idea of duty. But even duty is viewed by each in very different lights. The Church enjoins it as obedience to God, and the State enforces it as the safeguard of order. But there can be no collision, unless one or the other blunders as to the things that are materially right. When the State makes wicked laws, contradicting the eternal principles of rectitude, the Church is at liberty to testify against them; and humbly to petition that they may be repealed. In like manner, if the Church becomes seditious and a disturber of the peace, the State has a right to abate the nuisance. In ordinary cases, however, there is not likely to be a collision. Among a Christian people, there is little difference of opinion as to the radical distinctions of right and wrong. The only serious danger is where moral duty is conditioned upon a political question. Under the pretext of inculcating duty, the Church may usurp the power to determine the question which conditions it and that is precisely what she is debarred from doing. The condition must be given. She must accept it from the State, and then her own course is clear. If Cæsar is your master, then pay tribute to him; but whether the *if* holds, whether Cæsar is your master or not, whether he ever had any just authority, whether he now retains it, or has forfeited it, these are points which the Church has no commission to adjudicate.

Had these principles been steadily maintained by the Assembly at Philadelphia, it is possible that the ecclesiastical separation of the North and the South might have been deferred for years to come. Our Presbyteries, many of them, clung with tenderness to the recollections of the past. Sacred memories gathered around that venerable Church which had breasted many a storm and trained our fathers for glory. It had always been distinguished for its conservative influence, and many fondly hoped that, even in the present emergency, it would raise its placid and serene head above the tumults of popular passion, and bid defiance to the angry billows which rolled at its feet. We expected it to bow in reverence only at the name of Jesus. Many dreamed that it would utterly refuse to know either Confederates or Federalists, and utterly refuse to give any authoritative decree without a "thus saith the Lord." It was ardently desired that the sublime spectacle might be presented of one Church upon earth combining in cordial fellowship and in holy love the disciples of Jesus in different and even in hostile lands. But, alas! for the weakness of man, these golden visions were soon dispelled.

The first thing which roused our Presbyteries to look the question of separation seriously in the face, was the course of the Assembly in venturing to determine, as a Court of Jesus Christ, which it did by necessary implication, the true interpretation of the Constitution of the United States as to the kind of government it intended to form. A political theory was, to all intents and purposes, propounded, which made secession a crime, the seceding States rebellious, and the citizens who obeyed them traitors. We say nothing here as to the righteousness or unrighteousness of these decrees. What we maintain is, that whether right or wrong, the Church had no right to make them – she transcended her sphere, and usurped the duties of the State. The discussion of these questions, we are sorry to add, was in the spirit and temper of partizan declaimers. The Assembly, driven from its ancient moorings, was tossed to and fro by the waves of popular passion. Like

Pilate, it obeyed the clamor of the multitude, and though acting in the name of Jesus, it kissed the sceptre and bowed the knee to the mandates of Northern phrenzy. The Church was converted into the forum, and the Assembly was henceforward to become the arena of sectional divisions and national animosities.

We frankly admit that the mere unconstitutionality of the proceedings of the last Assembly is not, in itself considered, a sufficient ground of separation. It is the consequences of these proceedings which make them so offensive. It is the door which they open for the introduction of the worst passions of human nature into the deliberations of Church Courts. The spirit of these proceedings, if allowed to prevail, would forever banish peace from the Church, and there is no reason to hope that the tide which has begun to flow can soon be arrested. The two Confederacies hate each other more intensely now than they did in May and if their citizens should come together upon the same floor, whatever might be the errand that brought them there, they could not be restrained from smiting each other with the fist of wickedness. For the sake of peace, therefore, for Christian charity, for the honor of the Church, and for the glory of God, we have been constrained, as much as in us lies, to remove all occasion of offence. We have quietly separated, and we are grateful to God that while leaving for the sake of peace, we leave it with the humble consciousness that we, ourselves, have never given occasion to break the peace. We have never confounded Cæsar and Christ, and we have never mixed the issues of this world with the weighty matters that properly belong to us as citizens of the Kingdom of God.

2. Though the immediate occasion of separation was the course of the General Assembly at Philadelphia in relation to the Federal Government and the war, yet there is another ground on which the independent organization of the Southern Church can be amply and scripturally maintained. The unity of the Church does not require a formal bond of union among all the congregations of believers throughout the earth. It does not demand a vast imperial monarchy like that of Rome, nor a strictly universal council, like that to which the complete development of Presbyterianism would naturally give rise. The Church Catholic is one in Christ, but it is not necessarily one visible, all-absorbing organization upon earth. There is no schism where there is no breach of charity. Churches may be perfectly at one in every principle of faith and order, and yet geographically distinct, and mutually independent. As the unity of the human race is not disturbed by its division into countries and nations, so the unity of the spiritual seed of Christ is neither broken nor impaired by separation and division into various Church constitutions. Accordingly, in all Protestant countries, Church organizations have followed national lines. The Calvinistic Churches of Switzerland are distinct from the Reformed Church of France. The Presbyterians of Ireland belong to a different Church from the Presbyterians of Scotland, and the Presbyterians of this country constitute a Church, in like manner, distinct from all other Churches on the globe. That the division into national Churches – that is, Churches bounded by national lines – is, in the present condition of human nature, a benefit, seems to us too obvious for proof. It realizes to the Church Catholic all the advantages of a di-

vision of labor. It makes a Church organization homogeneous and compact – it stimulates holy rivalry and zeal – it removes all grounds of suspicion and jealousy on the part of the State. What is lost in expansion is gained in energy. The Church Catholic, as thus divided, and yet spiritually one; divided, but not rent, is a beautiful illustration of the great philosophical principle which pervades all nature – the co-existence of the one with the many.

If it is desirable that each nation should contain a separate and an independent Church, the Presbyteries of these Confederate States need no apology for bowing to the decree of Providence, which, in withdrawing their country from the Government of the United States, has, at the same time, determined that they should withdraw from the Church of their fathers. It is not that they have ceased to love it – not that they have abjured its ancient principles, or forgotten its glorious history. It is to give these same principles a richer, freer, fuller development among ourselves than they possibly could receive under foreign culture. It is precisely because we love that Church as it was, and that Church as it should be, that we have resolved, as far as in us lies, to realise its grand idea in the country, and under the Government where God has cast our lot. With the supreme control of ecclesiastical affairs in our own hands, we may be able, in some competent measure, to consummate this result. In subjection to a foreign power, we could no more accomplish it than the Church in the United States could have been developed in dependence upon the Presbyterian Church of Scotland. The difficulty there would have been, not the distance of Edinburgh from New York, Philadelphia or Charleston, but the difference in the manners, habits, customs and ways of thinking, the social, civil and political institutions of the people. These same difficulties exist in relation to the Confederate and United States, and render it eminently proper that the Church in each should be as separate and independent as the Governments.

In addition to this, there is one difference which so radically and fundamentally distinguishes the North and the South, that it is becoming every day more and more apparent that the religious, as well as the secular interests of both will be more effectually promoted by a complete and lasting separation. The antagonism of Northern and Southern sentiment on the subject of slavery lies at the root of all the difficulties which have resulted in the dismemberment of the Federal Union, and involved us in the horrors of an unnatural war. The Presbyterian Church in the United States has been enabled by the Divine grace to pursue, for the most part, an eminently conservative, because a thoroughly scriptural, policy in relation to this delicate question. It has planted itself upon the Word of God, and utterly refused to make slave-holding a sin, or non-slaveholding a term of communion. But though both sections are agreed as to this general principle, it is not to be disguised that the North exercises a deep and settled antipathy to slavery itself, while the South is equally zealous in its defence. Recent events can have no other effect than to confirm the antipathy on the one hand and strengthen the attachment on the other. The Northern section of the Church stands in the awkward predicament of maintaining, in one breath, that slavery is an evil which ought to be abolished, and of asserting, in the next, that it is not a sin to be visited

by exclusion from communion of the saints. The consequence is, that it plays partly into the hands of Abolitionists and partly into the hands of slaveholders, and weakens
its influence with both. It occupies the position of a prevar-
icating witness whom neither party will trust. It would be
better, therefore, for the moral power of the Northern section of the Church to get entirely quit of the subject. At the
same time, it is intuitively obvious that the Southern section of the Church, while even partially under the control
of those who are hostile to slavery, can never have free and
unimpeded access to the slave population. Its ministers
and elders will always be liable to some degree of suspicion. In the present circumstances, Northern alliance would
be absolutely fatal. It would utterly preclude the Church
from a wide and commanding field of usefulness. This is
too dear a price to be paid for a nominal union. We cannot
afford to give up these millions of souls and consign them,
so far as our efforts are concerned, to hopeless perdition,
for the sake of preserving an outward unity which, after
all, is an empty shadow. If we would gird ourselves heartily and in earnest, for the work which God has set before
us, we must have the control of our ecclesiastical affairs,
and declare ourselves separate and independent.

And here we may venture to lay before the Christian
world our views as a Church upon the subject of slavery.
We beg a candid hearing.

In the first place, we would have it distinctly understood that, in our ecclesiastical capacity, we are neither the
friends nor the foes of slavery; that is to say, we have no
commission either to propagate or abolish it. The policy of
its existence or non-existence is a question which exclusive-

ly belongs to the State. We have no right, as a Church, to enjoin it as a duty, or to condemn it as a sin. Our business is with the duties which spring from the relation; the duties of the masters on the one hand, and of their slaves on the other. These duties we are to proclaim and to enforce with spiritual sanctions. The social, civil, political problems connected with this great subject transcend our sphere, as God has not entrusted to His Church the organization of society, the construction of governments, nor the allotment of individuals to their various stations. The Church has as much right to preach to the monarchies of Europe, and the despotism of Asia, the doctrines of republican equality, as to preach to the governments of the South the extirpation of slavery. This position is impregnable, unless it can be shown that slavery is a sin. Upon every other hypothesis, it is so clearly a question for the State, that the proposition would never for a moment have been doubted, had there not been a foregone conclusion in relation to its moral character. Is slavery, then, a sin?

In answering this question, as a Church, let it be distinctly borne in mind that the only rule of judgment is the written Word of God. The Church knows nothing of the intuitions of reason or the deductions of philosophy, except those reproduced in the Sacred Canon. She has a positive constitution in the Holy Scriptures, and has no right to utter a single syllable upon any subject, except as the Lord puts words in her mouth. She is founded, in other words, upon express revelation. Her creed is an authoritative testimony of God, and not a speculation, and what she proclaims, she must proclaim with the infallible certitude of faith, and not with the hesitating assent of an opinion. The question, then, is brought within a narrow compass: Do the Scriptures directly or indirectly condemn slavery as a sin? If they do not, the dispute is ended, for the Church, without forfeiting her character, dares not go beyond them.

Now, we venture to assert that if men had drawn their conclusions upon this subject only from the Bible, it would no more have entered into any human head to denounce slavery as a sin, than to denounce monarchy, aristocracy or poverty. The truth is, men have listened to what they falsely considered as primitive intuitions, or as necessary deductions from primitive cognitions, and then have gone to the Bible to confirm the crotchets of their vain philosophy. They have gone there determined to find a particular result, and the consequence is, that they leave with having made, instead of having interpreted, Scripture. Slavery is no new thing. It has not only existed for ages in the world, but it has existed, under every dispensation of the covenant of grace, in the Church of God. Indeed, the first organization of the Church as a visible society, separate and distinct from the unbelieving world, was inaugurated in the family of a slaveholder. Among the very first persons to whom the seal of circumcision was affixed, were the slaves of the father of the faithful, some born in his house, and others bought with his money. Slavery again re-appears under the Law. God sanctions it in the first table of the Decalogue, and Moses treats it as an institution to be regulated, not abolished; legitimated and not condemned. We come down to the age of the New Testament, and we find it again in the Churches founded by the Apostles under the plenary inspiration of the Holy Ghost. These facts are utterly amazing if slavery is the enormous sin which its enemies represent it to be. It will not do to say that the Scriptures have treated it only in a general, incidental way, without any clear implication as to its moral character. Moses surely made it the subject of express and positive legislation, and the Apostles are equally explicit in inculcating the duties which spring from both sides of the relation. They treat slaves as bound to obey and inculcate obedience as an office of religion – a thing wholly self-contradictory, if the authority exercised over them were unlawful and iniquitous.

But what puts this subject in a still clearer light, is the manner in which it is sought to extort from the Scriptures a contrary testimony. The notion of direct and explicit condemnation is given up. The attempt is to show that the genius and spirit of Christianity are opposed to it – that its great cardinal principles of virtue are utterly against it. Much stress is laid upon the Golden Rule and upon the general denunciations of tyranny and oppression. To all this we reply, that no principle is clearer than that a case positively excepted cannot be included under a general rule. Let us concede, for a moment, that the laws of love, and the condemnation of tyranny and oppression, seem logically to involve, as a result, the condemnation of slavery; yet, if slavery is afterwards expressly mentioned and treated as a lawful relation, it obviously follows, unless Scripture is to be interpreted as inconsistent with itself, that slavery is, by necessary implication, excepted. The Jewish law forbade, as a general rule, the marriage of a man with his brother's wife. The same law expressly enjoined the same marriage in a given case. The given case was, therefore, an exception, and not to be treated as a violation of the general rule. The law of love has always been the law of God. It was enunciated by Moses almost as clearly as it was enunciated by Jesus Christ. Yet, notwithstanding this law, Moses and the Apostles alike sanctioned the relation of slavery. The conclusion is inevitable, either that the law is not opposed to it, or that slavery is an excepted case. To say that the prohibition of tyranny and oppression include slavery, is to beg the whole question. Tyranny and oppression involve either the unjust usurpation or the unlawful exercise of power. It is the unlawfulness, either in its principle or measure, which constitutes the core of the sin. Slavery must, therefore, be proved to be unlawful, before it can be referred to any such category. The master may, indeed, abuse his power, but he oppresses not simply as a master, but as a wicked master.

But, apart from all this, the law of love is simply the inculcation of universal equity. It implies nothing as to the existence of various ranks and gradations in society. The interpretation which makes it repudiate slavery would make it equally repudiate all social, civil and political inequalities. Its meaning is, not that we should conform ourselves to the arbitrary expectations of others, but that we should render unto them precisely the same measure which, if we were in their circumstances, it would be reasonable and just in us to demand at their hands. It condemns slavery, therefore, only upon the supposition that slavery is a sinful relation – that is, he who extracts the prohibition of slavery from the Golden Rule, begs the very point in dispute.

We cannot prosecute the argument in detail, but we have said enough we think, to vindicate the position of the

Southern Church. We have assumed no new attitude. We stand exactly were the Church of God has always stood – from Abraham to Moses, from Moses to Christ, from Christ to the Reformers, and from the Reformers to ourselves. We stand upon the foundation of the Prophets and Apostles, Jesus Christ Himself being the Chief corner stone. Shall we be excluded from the fellowship of our brethren in other lands, because we dare not depart from the charter of our faith? Shall we be branded with the stigma of reproach, because we cannot consent to corrupt the Word of God to suit the intuitions of an infidel philosophy? Shall our names be cast out as evil, and the finger of scorn pointed at us, because we utterly refuse to break our communion with Abraham, Isaac and Jacob, with Moses, David and Isaiah, with Apostles, Prophets and Martyrs, with all the noble army of confessors who have gone to glory from slave-holding countries and from a slave-holding Church, without ever having dreamed that they were living in mortal sin, by conniving at slavery in the midst of them? If so, we shall take consolation in the cheering consciousness that the Master has accepted us. We may be denounced, despised and cast out of the Synagogues of our brethren. But while they are wrangling about the distinctions of men according to the flesh, we shall go forward in our Divine work, and confidently anticipate that, in the great day, as the consequence of our humble labors, we shall meet millions of glorified spirits, who have come up from the bondage of earth to a nobler freedom than human philosophy ever dreamed of. Others, if they please, may spend their time in declaiming on the tyranny of earthly masters; it will be our aim to resist the real tyrants which oppress the soul – Sin and Satan. These are the foes against whom we shall find it employment enough to wage a successful war. And to this holy war it is the purpose of our Church to devote itself with redoubled energy. We feel that the souls of our slaves are a solemn trust, and we shall strive to present them faultless and complete before the presence of God.

Indeed, as we contemplate their condition in the Southern States, and contrast it with that of their fathers before them, and that of their brethren in the present day in their native land, we cannot but accept it as a gracious Providence that they have been brought in such numbers to our shores, and redeemed from the bondage of barbarism and sin. Slavery to them has certainly been overruled for the greatest good. It has been a link in the wondrous chain of Providence, through which many sons and daughters have been made heirs of the heavenly inheritance. The providential result is, of course, no justification, if the thing is intrinsically wrong; but it is certainly a matter of devout thanksgiving, and no obscure intimation of the will and purpose of God, and of the consequent duty of the Church. We cannot forbear to say, however, that the general operation of the system is kindly and benevolent; it is a real and effective discipline, and without it, we are profoundly persuaded that the African race in the midst of us can never be elevated in the scale of being. As long as that race, in its comparative degradation, co-exists, side by side, with the White, bondage is its normal condition.

As to the endless declamation about human rights, we have only to say that human rights are not a fixed, but a fluctuating quantity. Their sum is not the same in any two nations on the globe. The rights of Englishmen are one thing; the rights of Frenchmen another. There is a minimum without which a man cannot be responsible; there is a maximum which expresses the highest degree of civilization and of Christian culture. The education of the species consists in its ascent along this line. As you go up, the number of rights increases, but the number of individuals who possess them diminishes. As you come down the line, rights are diminished, but the individuals are multiplied. It is just the opposite of the predicamental scale of the logicians. There comprehension diminishes as you ascend and extension increases, and comprehension increases as you descend and extension diminishes. Now, when it is said that slavery is inconsistent with human rights, we crave to understand what point in this line is the slave conceived to occupy. There are, no doubt, many rights which belong to other men – to Englishmen, to Frenchmen, to his master, for example – which are denied to him. But is he fit to possess them? Has God qualified him to meet the responsibilities which their possession necessarily implies? His place in the scale is determined by his competency to fulfil its duties. There are other rights which he certainly possesses, without which he could neither be human nor accountable. Before slavery can be charged with doing him injustice, it must be shown that the minimum which falls to his lot at the bottom of the line is out of proportion to his capacity and culture — a thing which can never be done by abstract speculation. The truth is, the education of the human race for liberty and virtue, is a vast providential scheme, and God assigns to every man, by a wise and holy decree, the precise place he is to occupy in the great moral school of humanity. The scholars are distributed into classes, according to their competency and progress. For God is in history.

To avoid the suspicion of a conscious weakness of our cause, when contemplated from the side of pure speculation, we may advert for a moment to those pretended intuitions which stamp the reprobation of humanity upon this ancient and hoary institution. We admit that there are primitive principles in morals which lie at the root of human consciousness. But the question is, how are we to distinguish them? The subjective feeling of certainty is no adequate criterion, as that is equally felt in reference to crotchets and hereditary prejudices. The very point is to know when this certainty indicates a primitive cognition, and when it does not. There must, therefore, be some eternal test, and whatever cannot abide that test has no authority as a primary truth. That test is an inward necessity of thought, which, in all minds at the proper stage of maturity, is absolutely universal. Whatever is universal is natural. We are willing that slavery should be tried by this standard. We are willing to abide by the testimony of the race, and if man, as man, has every where condemned it – if all human laws have prohibited it as crime – if it stands in the same category with malice, murder and theft, then we are willing, in the name of humanity, to renounce it, and to renounce it forever. But what if the overwhelming majority of mankind have approved it? What if philosophers and statesmen have justified it, and the laws of all nations acknowledged it; what then becomes of these luminous intuitions? They are an *ignis fatuus* – mistaken for a star.

We have now, brethren, in a brief compass – for the nature of this address admits only of an outline – opened to you our whole hearts upon this delicate and vexed subject. We have concealed nothing. We have sought to conciliate no sympathy by appeals to your charity. We have tried our cause by the Word of God; and though protesting against its authority to judge in a question concerning the duty of the Church, we have not refused to appear at the tribunal of reason. Are we not right, in view of all the preceding considerations, in remitting the social, civil and political problems connected with slavery to the State? Is it not a subject, save in the moral duties which spring from it, which lies beyond the province of the Church? Have we any right to make it an element in judging of Christian character? Are we not treading in the footsteps of the flock? Are we are not acting as Christ and His Apostles have acted before us? Is it not enough for us to pray and labor, in our lot, that all men may be saved, without meddling as a Church with the technical distinction of their civil life? We leave the matter with you. We offer you the right hand of fellowship. It is for you to accept it or reject it. We have done our duty. We can do no more. Truth is more precious than union, and if you cast us out as sinners, the breach of charity is not with us, as long as we walk according to the light of the written Word.

The ends which we propose to accomplish as a Church are the same as those which are proposed by every other Church. To proclaim God's truth as a witness to the nations; to gather His elect from the four corners of the earth, and through the Word, Ministries and Ordinances to train them for eternal life, is the great business of His people. The only thing that will be at all peculiar to us, is the manner in which we shall attempt to discharge our duty. In almost every department of labor, except the pastoral care of congregations, it has been usual for the Church to resort to societies more or less closely connected with itself, and yet, logically and really distinct. It is our purpose to rely upon the regular organs of our government, and executive agencies directly and immediately responsible to them. We wish to make the Church, not merely a superintendent, but an agent. We wish to develop the idea that the congregation of believers, as visibly organized, is the very society or corporation which is divinely called to do the work of the Lord. We shall, therefore, endeavor to do what has never yet been adequately done – bring out the energies of our Presbyterian system of government. From the Session to the Assembly we shall strive to enlist all our courts, as courts, in every department of Christian effort. We are not ashamed to confess that we are intensely Presbyterian. We embrace all other denominations in the arms of Christian fellowship and love, but our own scheme of government we humbly believe to be according to the pattern shown in the Mount, and, by God's grace, we propose to put its efficiency to the test.

Brethren, we have done. We have told you who we are, and what we are. We greet you in the ties of Christian brotherhood. We desire to cultivate peace and charity with all our fellow Christians throughout the world. We invite to ecclesiastical communion all who maintain our principles of faith and order. And now we commend you to God and the Word of His grace. We devoutly pray that the whole Catholic Church may be afresh baptised with the Holy Ghost, and that she may speedily be stirred up to give the Lord no rest until He establish and make Jerusalem a praise in the earth.

The above document was adopted unanimously by the First General Assembly of the Presbyterian Church in the Confederate States of America, held at Augusta, Georgia in December, 1861. It was written by J. H. Thornwell, and signed by B. M. Palmer, moderator, Jonathan N. Waddel, stated clerk, Joseph R. Wilson, permanent clerk, and D. McNeill Turner, temporary clerk, as well as by 46 ministers and 33 ruling elders of the denomination. The PCCSA would later become the Presbyterian Church in the United States (PCUS) after the overthrow of the Southern Confederacy in 1865.

VI

Letter to Gen. Oliver O. Howard, U.S. Freedmen's Bureau, Regarding Care of the Former Slaves
by Rev. Robert Lewis Dabney, D.D., LL.D.

Prince Edward County, Virginia
12 September 1865.

Sir: Your high official trust makes you, in a certain sense, the representative man of the North, as concerns their dealing with the African race in these United States. It is as such that I venture to address you, and through you all your fellow-citizens on behalf of this recently liberated people. My purpose is humbly to remind you of your weighty charge, and to encourage you to go forward with an enlarged philanthropy and zeal in that career of beneficence toward the African which Providence has opened before you. Rarely has it fallen to the lot of one of the sons of men to receive a larger trust, or to enjoy a wider opportunity for doing good. At the beginning of the late war there were in the South nearly four millions of Africans. All these, a nation in numbers, now taken from their former guardians, are laid upon the hands of that government of which you are the special agent for their protection and guidance. To this nation of Black people you are virtually father and king; your powers for their management are unlimited, and for assisting their needs you have the resources of the "greatest people on earth." Your action for the freedmen's good is restrained by no constitution or precedents, but the powers you exercise for them are as full as your office is novel. We see evidence of this in the fact that your agents, acting for the good of your charge, can seize by military arrest any one of their fellow-citizens of African descent, for no other offense than being unemployed, convey him without his consent, and without the company of his wife and family, to a distant field of industry, where he is compelled to wholesome labor for such remuneration as you may be pleased to assign. Another evidence is seen in your late order, transferring all causes and indictments in which a freedman is a party, from the courts of law of the Southern States to the bar of your own commissioners and sub-commissioners for adjudication. I beg you to believe that these instances are not cited by me for the purpose of repeating the cavils against the justice and consistency of the powers exercised in them, in which some have been heard to indulge. My purpose is not to urge with them that there is no law by which a free citizen can be rightfully abridged of his liberty of enjoying the *otium cum dignitate* so long as he abstains from crime or misdemeanor therein, merely because he wears a Black skin, while the same government does not presume to interfere with the exercise of this privilege by his White fellow-citizens, even though they be those lately in rebellion against it; that this military arrest and transference to the useful though distant scene of compulsory labor, is precisely that penalty of "transportation" which Southern laws never inflicted, even on the slave, except for crime and after judicial investigation; that these commissioners for adjudicating cases to which freedmen are parties, are in reality judges at law, appointed by you, for every city and county in eleven States, and empowered to sit without jury, and to decide without regard to the precedents or statutes of the States; which would exhibit your bureau as not only an executive, but a judicial branch of the government, established without constitutional authority, and that a hundred fold more pervasive in its jurisdiction than the Supreme Court itself; and that this "order" has, by one stroke of your potent pen, deprived eight millions of White people of the right of a trial by jury, guaranteed to them by the sixth and seventh additional articles of the United States Constitution, in every case where a freedman happens to be a party against them. I repeat, that I have not adduced these instances for the purpose of urging these or such like objections (it does not become the subject to cavil against the powers exercised by his conquerors), but only to impress you with the obligation, which the fullness of your powers brings upon you, to do good to your charge upon a great scale.

I cannot believe that means will be lacking to you any more than powers. At your back stands the great, the powerful, the rich, the prosperous, the philanthropic, the Christian North, friend and liberator of the Black man. It must be assumed that the zeal which waged a gigantic war for four years, which expended three thousand million of dollars, and one million of lives, in large part to free the African, will be willing to lavish anything else which may be needed for his welfare. And if the will be present, the ability is no less abundant among a people so wealthy and powerful, who exhibit the unprecedented spectacle of an emersion from a war which would have been exhausting to any other people with resources larger than when they began it, and who have found out (what all previous statesmen deemed an impossibility), that the public wealth may be actually increased by unproductive consumption. With full powers and means to do everything for the African, what may he not expect from your guardianship?

The answer which a generous and humane heart would make to this question, must of course be this: that it would seek to do for the good of its charge *everything which is possible*. But more definitely I wish to remind you that there is a *minimum* limit, which the circumstances of the case forbid you to touch. Common sense, common justice says: that *the very least you can do for them must be more than the South has accomplished*, from whose tutelage they have been taken. To this measure, at least, if not to some higher, your country, posterity, fame, and the righteous heavens, will rigidly hold you. The reason is almost too plain to be explained. If a change procured for the Africans at such a cost brings them no actual benefit, then that cost is uncompensated, and the expenditure of human weal which has been made was a blunder and a crime. Thus it becomes manifest that the measure for the task which you have before you, is the work which the South accomplished for the Negro while he was a slave. The question, how much was this? is a vital one for you; it gives you your starting point from which you must advance in your career of progressive philanthropy. Listen then.

First, for the physical welfare of the Negro the South has done something. A rapid increase of population and longevity are a safe index of the prosperous and sane condition of the bodies of a people. The South has so provided for the wants of the Negro that his numbers have doubled themselves as rapidly as those of the Whites, with no accessions by immigration. The census returns show that the South so cared for him that the percentage of congenital defects and diseases, these unfailing revealers of a depressed physical condition, idiocy, blindness, deafness, dumbness, hereditary scrofula, and such like ills, was as small as among the most prosperous Northern States. The South gave to her Negro men, on an average, a half pound of bacon and three pounds of breadstuffs per day, besides his share in the products of his master's kitchen-garden, dairy and orchard; and to the women and children at a rate equally liberal. If, in some neighborhoods, the supply was less bountiful than the above, there were a hundred fold more in which it was even more abundant. The South gave to every Negro, great and small, a pair of shoes every winter, and to the laboring men an additional pair at harvest. She clothed them all with a substantial suit of woolens every winter, an additional suit of cotton or flax each summer, and two shirts and two pair of socks per year, while the adults drew their hat and blanket each. She furnished each Negro family with a separate cottage or cabin, and, during the severe weather, with about one-third of a cord of wood per day, to keep up those liberal fires on which his health and life so much depend.

She provided, universally, such relief for his sickness that every case of serious disease was attended by a physician with nearly the same promptitude and frequency as the cases of the planters' own wives and daughters; and in all the land never was a Negro fastened to his bed by illness but he received the personal, sympathizing visits of some intelligent White person besides; master, mistress or their agent, who never went to his couch empty-handed. His dead universally received decent and Christian burial, where the bereaved survivors were soothed by the offices of Christianity. The South so shielded the Negro against destitution, that from the Potomac to the Gulf, not one Negro pauper was ever seen, unless he were free, and not one African poorhouse existed or was needed. Her system secured for every slave, male or female, a legal claim upon the whole property, income, and personal labor of his master, for a comfortable maintenance during any season of infirmity brought upon him by old age, the visitation of God, or his own imprudence, however protracted that season might be: a claim so sure and definite that it could be pursued by an action at law upon the slave's behalf; a claim so universally enforced and acquiesced in, that its neglect, or the death of a helpless slave through destitution, was as completely unknown among us as cannibalism.

The South met that claim, which the free laboring men of other lands have so often had sorrowful occasion to argue, amid pallid famine, and with the fearful logic of insurrections and bloodshed, the claim of "the right to labor," and has met it so successfully that she has secured to every African slave capable of labor, without even one exception among all her millions, remunerative occupation, at all times, and amid all financial convulsions and depressions of business. That is, she has found at all times such occupation for all of them as has procured for them, without excessive toil, a decent maintenance during their active years, an adequate and unfailing provision for old age, a portion for their widows, and a rearing of their children. The South has so far performed these duties to the bodies of the Africans that no community of them have ever, in a single instance, amid any war, or blight, or drouth, or dearth, felt the tooth of famine on its vitals, or so much as seen the wolf, destitution, at its door.

For the culture of the Negro's mind and character, the South has also done something. She has not, indeed, fallen into the hallucination that the only processes of education are those summed up in the arts of reading and writing – facts which were not prevalent among those literacy dictators of the ancient world, the compatriots of Pericles and Plato – nor has she deemed it a likely mode to communicate these useful acts to the ebony youth, to gather three hundred of them into one pandemonium, under a single overtasked "school-marm" or bald-pated Negro, and dub the seething cauldron of noise, confusion and "Negro-gen gas," a "primary school." But thousands and tens of thousands has she taught to read (and offered the art to ten-fold more, who declined it from their own indolence), through the gentle and faithful agency of cultivated young masters and mistresses, a process prohibited, I boldly assert, *quicunque vult*, by no law upon the statute-book of my State, at least. But this tuition, extensive as it has been, is

the merest atom and mite, in the extensive culture which
she has given to the African race. She received them at the
hands of British and Yankee slave traders, besotted in their
primeval jungles, for the spontaneous fruits of which they
lived in common. She taught the whole of them some rudi-
ments of civilization. She taught them all the English language, a gift which, had they been introduced into the
Northern States as free men, in numbers so large, they
would not have received in three centuries. She taught all
of them some arts of useful labor, and as large a portion of
them as any other peasantry learned the mechanical arts.
With the comparatively small exception of the Negroes
upon large estates, belonging to non-resident owners, the
South has placed every Negro boy and girl, during his or
her growth, under the forming influence of White men and
ladies, by whom they have been taught some little tinctures
of the cleanliness, the decencies, the chastity, the truthful-
ness, the self-respect, so utterly alien to their former savage
condition, and a share of courtesy and good breeding
which would not disgrace any civilized people. Of the
young Negresses, who would otherwise have grown up
the besotted victims of brutal passions, the great majority
have been, at some stage of their training, introduced by
the South to the parlors and chambers of their women,
from whom they have learned to revere and imitate, to
some degree, that grace and purity, that sweet humanity
and delicacy of sentiment which glorify the Southern lady
above all her sex; and under her watchful and kindly eye,
has her dark-skinned sister been taught the agencies and
domestic arts which make woman a blessing in her home.
The boys and youths, by the same influences, have become

the humble, yet affectionate, companions of their masters, and have imbibed some of their intelligence and principle. Herein was the great educational work of the South, potent and persuasive as it was simple. By her system, every man and woman of the superior race, yea, every child, was enlisted in the work of the culture of the inferior, and the whole business of domestic life was converted, by interest and affection alike, into a schooling of the mind and character.

This culture has been so far successful that the African race, lately rude savages, was raised to such a grade that, according to high military authority in the United States, they were fit to make armies as efficient as those recruited in the "great, free and enlightened North"; and in the judgment of a powerful party in that country (a party which embraces the major part of that particular corner which has the prescriptive right of knowing everything), they have been made, under Southern tutelage, fully equal to the rights and duties of voters and rulers, in the most complicated of governments. Now, feeling that it does not become a subject of that government, one recently conquered by the great North, to dispute its *dicta* on these points, I shall of course assume that they are correct. Here, then, is what the South has done for the development of the Negro's mind.

Nor has our section neglected that noblest and highest interest of all races – the spiritual interest of the Negro. She has diffused among the Blacks a pure Gospel. She gave him the Christian Sabbath, and fortified the gift with laws and penalties, capable of being executed in his behalf against his own master – laws so efficacious that enforced Sabbath labor was almost utterly unknown to him. She gave him a part in every house of worship built throughout her border (for never have I heard of one church in all these States where the slaves were not admitted along with their masters), besides building more temples for his exclusive use than the Christianity of the North has built for Pagans in all Hindostan and China together. She has given him evangelical preaching, unmingled with the poison of Universalism, Millerism, Socinianism, Mormonism, or with the foreign and disastrous element of politics. For nearly all the church-members of this people are connected with the great orthodox and evangelical denominations; and having been a preacher to Africans for twenty years, I have never yet heard a sermon addressed to them, or heard of the man who had heard it, in which the subject of abolition or pro-slavery was obtruded on their attention by a Southern minister. In one word, the South has so far cared for their souls as to bring five hundred thousand of them into the full communion of the Church, thus making them at least outward and professed Christians – a ratio as large as that prevailing among the Whites of the great, Christian North.

These facts concerning the work of the South for the slaves, I give without the fear of contradiction. The son of a slaveholder, an owner of slaves by inheritance, reared and educated among them, laboring for them and their masters all my professional life, I know whereof I affirm. Every intelligent citizen of the South will substantiate these statements, as within the limits of moderation, and as only a part of those which might be made.

When I claim that the South did thus much for the Africans, I am far from boasting. We ought to have done much more. Instead of pointing to it with self-laudation, it becomes us, with profound humility towards God, to confess our shortcomings towards our servants. He has been pleased, in His sovereign and fearful dispensation, to lay upon us a grievous affliction, and we know He is too just to do this except for our sins. While I am as certain as the sure word of Scripture can make me concerning any principle of social duty, that there was nothing sinful in the relation of master and slave itself, I can easily believe that our failure to fulfill some of the duties of that righteous relation is among the sins for which God's hand now makes us smart. And it does not become those who are under His discipline to boast of their good works. No; verily we have sinned; my arguments is that you must do more for the Negro than we sinners of the South have done.

I have written wittingly the words, *you* must do it for them. The South cannot. Your people have effectually disabled them therefor. They have done so by taking away our wealth. The South is almost utterly impoverished, and is able to do little more than to keep destitution from her own doors. But a more conclusive reason is the alienation which the armed and clerical missionaries of the North have inculcated in the breasts of these people, lately so affectionate and contented. The Negroes have been diligently taught that their masters were their enemies and oppressors, that their bondage was wicked and destructive of their well-being, and especially that the religious teachings of all Southern ministers were "doctrines of devils," because they would not shout the shibboleth of abolition. The consequence is that the Black race will no longer listen to the Southern people, or be guided by them. Take as evi-

dence my own instance, which I cite precisely for the reason that it is not in the least peculiar, but reflects the common experience of all ministers and people here. Before the
advent of your armies, plantation meetings were held
weekly in the different quarters of the congregation, on
Saturdays, in working time, cheerfully surrendered by the
masters for that purpose, which brought religious instruction within two or three miles of every house. They are
now all at an end. Six years ago my congregation pulled
down the substantial house, built by their fathers only thirty years before, with walls as solid as living rocks, which
was entirely adequate to hold the Whites, and replaced it
by a larger. One prominent reason was that it was not
large enough to hold the servants also. They constructed in
the new house three hundred commodious sittings exclusively for the Blacks. Last Sabbath, under a bright and
cheerful sun, those sittings were occupied during public
worship by precisely three persons; and at the afternoon
service, held in a chapel-of-ease, primarily for the Blacks,
there was not one present. Thus the North has prevented
the South from doing its former work for the good of the
African; consequently it must make its account to do it all
itself.

But while I assert this, I would bear my emphatic testimony against the falsehood and injustice of the charge that
the Southern people wish to cast off and ruin the Negro, in
a spirit of pique and revenge for his emancipation. That
they regard this measure as neither just nor wise, is perfectly true. But they have promised to acquiesce in it as a
condition of peace; that promise they intend faithfully to
keep; and they universally regard slavery as finally at an

end. There is nothing more manifest than that the North, amid the flame and heat of all its animosities, knows and feels that this people will not be the one to break its new covenant, hard as its conditions are; and that the freedom of the late slaves and the authority which has dictated it are secured from attack by us. And I boldly testify that this magnanimous people has not voluntarily withdrawn its humane interest from the Blacks; that it earnestly desires their prosperity; that it wishes to give them employment and opportunity, and to co-operate in their maintenance as far as possible; that they do not cast off the Negroes, but it is the Negroes who cast them off. Yea, the people of the South are this day extending to tens of thousands of Black families a generous sympathy in the midst of their own heavy losses and deep poverty, which we challenge the Christian world to surpass in its splendid philanthropy: in that we still refuse to cast off those families, although, by reason of the incumbrance of old persons, sick, and little children, their present labor is worse than worthless to us, and we know we shall receive no future recompense in the labor of the children we are thus rearing *gratis* for other men as independent of us in future as we are of them. And this is done (oftentimes in spite of a present requital of insolence, misconception, ingratitude and a petty warfare of thefts and injuries) by Southern gentlemen and ladies, who appropriate thereto a part of the avails of their own personal labors, undertaken to procure subsistence for their own children. And this is done, not in a few exceptional cases, but in a multitude of cases, in every neighborhood of every county, so that the numbers of destitute freedmen under which the able hands of your Bureau now faint, are

not a tithe of those who are still maintained by the impoverished people of the South. And this is done simply because humanity makes us unwilling to thrust out those for
whose happiness we have so long been accustomed to care
into the hardships of their new and untried future. And
unless you can expect this delicate sentiment to exhibit a
permanence which would be almost miraculous under the
"wear and tear" of our future poverty, I forewarn you that
you must stand prepared for a tenfold increase of your
present responsibilities, when these families are committed
to you. That tenfold burden you must learn to bear successfully.

Having shown you the starting point of that career of
beneficence to the African, from which you are solemnly
bound to God and history to advance, I now return to
strengthen the already irresistible argument of that obligation. If the South, with all its disadvantages, has done this
modicum of good to this poor people, the North, their
present guardian, with their vast advantages, must do far
more. The South was the inferior section (so the North told
us) in number, in wealth, in progress, in intelligence, in
education, in religion. The South (so the North says) held
the African under an antiquated, unrighteous and mischie-
vous relation – that of domestic slavery. The North now
has them on the new footing, which is, of course, precisely
the right one. The South was their oppressor; the North is
their generous liberator. The South was hagridden in all its
energies for good (so we were instructed) by the "barbarism of slavery"; the North contains the most civilized,
enlightened and efficient people on earth. Now, if you do
not surpass our poor performance for the Negro with this

mighty contrast in your favor, how mightily will be the just reprobation which will be visited upon you by the common sentiment of mankind and by the Lord of Hosts? If you do not surpass our deeds as far as your power and greatness surpass ours, how can you stand at His bar, even beside us sinners? He has taught us that "a man is accepted according to that which he hath, and not according to that which he hath not." To this righteous rule we intend to hold you, as our successors in the guardianship of the Negro.

If there are any who endeavor to lull your energies in this work, by saying that the Negro, being now a free man, must take care of himself like other people; that he should be thrown on his own resources, and that, if he does not provide for his own well-being, he should be left to suffer, I beseech you, in the behalf of humanity, of justice and of your own good name, not to hearken to them. I ask you solemnly whether the freedmen have an "even start" in the race for subsistence with the other laboring men of the nation, marked as they are by difference of race and color, obstructed by stubborn prejudices, and disqualified (as you hold) for the responsibilities of self-support, to some extent, by the evil effects of their recent bondage upon their character? Is it fair, or right, or merciful to compel him to enter the *stadium*, and leave him to this fierce competition under these grave disadvantages? Again, no peasantry under the sun was ever required or was ever able to sustain themselves when connected with the soil by no tenure of any form. Under our system, our slaves had the most permanent and beneficial form of tenancy; for their master's lands were bound to them by law for furnishing them homes, occupations and subsistence during the whole continuance of the master's tenure. But you have ended all this, and consigned four millions of people to a condition of homelessness. Will the North thus make gypsies of them, and then hold them responsible for the ruin which is inevitable from such a condition?

But there is another argument equally weighty. By adopting the unfeeling policy of throwing the Negro upon his own resources, to sink or swim as he may, you run too great a risk of verifying the most biting reproaches and objections of your enemies. They, in case of his failure, will argue thus: That the great question in debate between the defenders of slavery and the advocates of emancipation was whether the Negro was capable of self-control: that the former, who professed to be more intimately acquainted with his character, denied that he was capable of it, and solemnly warned you of the danger of his ruin, if he was intrusted with his own direction in this country, and that you, in insisting on the experiment in spite of this warning, assumed the whole responsibility. Sir, if the freedmen should perchance fail to swim successfully, that argument would be too damaging to you and your people. You cannot afford to venture upon this risk. You are compelled by the interests of your own consistency and good name, to take effectual care that the Negro shall swim; and that better than before. In the name of justice, I remonstrate against your throwing him off in his present state, by the inexorable fact that he was translated into it, neither by us, nor by himself, but by you alone; for out of that fact proceeds an obligation upon you, to make your experiment successful, which will cleave to you even to the judgment day. And out of that fact proceeds this farther obligation:

that seeing you have persisted, of your own free will, in making this experiment of his liberation, you and your people are bound to bestow anything or everything, and to do everything, except sin, to insure that it shall be, as compared with his previous condition, a blessing to him. For, if you are not willing to do all this, were you not bound to let him alone? When the shipmaster urges landsmen to embark in his ship, and venture the perils of the deep, he thereby incurs an obligation, if a storm arises, to do everything and risk everything, even to his own life, for the rescue of his charge. If, then, you and your people should find that it will require the labors of another million of busy hands, and the expenditure of three thousand millions more of the national wealth, to obviate the evils and dangers arising to the freedmen from your experiment upon their previous condition: yea, if to do this, it is necessary to make the care and maintenance of the African the sole business and labor of the whole mighty North, you will be bound to do it at this cost.

And I beg you, sir, let no one vainly think to evade this duty which they owe you in your charge, by saying that perhaps even so profuse an expenditure as this, for the benefit of the Africans, would fail of its object; because they hold that making a prosperous career is one of those things like chewing their own food, or repenting of their own sins, which people must do for themselves, or else they are impossible to be done; and that so no amount of help can make the freedmen prosperous as such, without the right putting forth of their own spontaneity. For, do you not see that this plea surrenders you into the hands of those bitter adversaries, the Pro-Slavery men? Is this not the very thing they said? This was precisely their argument to show that philanthropy required the Africans in this country should be kept in a dependent condition. If your section acquiesces in the failure of your experiment of their liberation on this ground, what will this be but the admission of the damning charge that your measure is a blunder and a crime, aggravated by the warning so emphatic, which your opponents gave you, and to which you refused to listen?

But I feel bound, as your zealous and faithful supporter in your humane task, to give you one more caution. The objectors who watch you with so severe an eye have even a darker suggestion to make than the charge of headstrong rashness and criminal mistake in your experiment of emancipation. They are heard gloomily to insinuate that the ruin of the African (which they so persistently assert must result from the change) is not the blunder of the North, but the foreseen and intended result! Are you aware of the existence of this frightful innuendo? It is my duty to reveal it to you, that you may be put upon your guard. These stern critics are heard darkly hinting that they know Northern statesmen and presses who now admit, with a sardonic shrug, that the Black man, deprived of the benignant shield of domestic servitude, must of course perish like the Red man. These critics are heard inferring that the true meaning of Northern Republicanism and Free Soil is, that the White race must be free to shoulder the Black race off this continent, and monopolize the sunny soil, which the God of nations gave the latter as their heritage. They take a sort of grim pleasure in pointing to the dead infants, which, they say, usually marked the liberating course of your armies through the South, in displaying the destitution and mortality which, they charge, are permitted in the vast settlements of freedmen under your care; in insinuating the rumors of official returns of a mortality already incurred in the Southwest, made to your government, so hideous that their suppression was a necessity; and in relating how the jungles which are encroaching upon the once smiling "coasts" of the Mississippi, in Louisiana, already envelope the graves of half the Black population in that State! And the terrible inference from all this, which they intimate is, that the great and powerful North only permits these disasters because it intends them; that, not satisfied with the wide domain which Providence has assigned to them, they now pretend to liberate the slave whom they have seen too prosperous under his domestic servitude, in order to destroy him, and grasp, in addition, the soil which he has occupied.

Now, sir, it is incumbent on you, that the premises on which, with so dangerous a plausibility, they ground this tremendous charge, be effectually contradicted by happy and beneficent results. You must refute this monstrous indictment, and there is only one way to do it: by actually showing that you conserve and bless the African race, multiply their numbers, and confirm their prosperity on the soil, more than we have done. I repeat, the North must refute it thus. For, of course, every Northern man, while indignantly denying and abhorring it, admits (what is as plain as the sun at midday) that if the charge were indeed true, it would convict his people of the Blackest public crime of the nineteenth century; a crime which would be found to involve every aggravation and every element of enormity which the nomenclature of ethics enables us to describe. It would be the deliberate, calculated, cold-blooded, selfish dedication of an innocent race of four millions to annihilation; the murder, with malice prepence, of a nation; not by the comparatively merciful process of the royal Hun, whose maxim was, that "thick grass is cut more easily than thin," summary massacre; but by the slowly eating cancer of destitution, degradation, immorality, protracting the long agony through two or three generations, thus multiplying the victims who would be permitted to be born only to sin, to suffer and to perish; and insuring the everlasting perdition of the soul, along with the body, by cunningly making their own vices the executioners of the doom. It would include the blackest guilt of treason being done under the deceitful mask of benefaction and by pretended liberators. The unrighteousness of its motive would concur with its treachery to enhance its guilt to the most stupendous height; for upon this interpretation of the purpose of the North, that motive would be, first to weaken and disable its late adversary, the South, by destroying that part of the people which was guilty of no sin against you, and then, by this union of fraud and force, to seize and enjoy the space which God gave them, and laws and Constitution guaranteed. This, indeed, would be the picture which these accusers would then present of your splendid act, that you came as a pretended friend and deliverer to the African, and while he embraced you as his benefactor in all his simple confidence and joy, you thrust your sword through and through his heart, in order to reach, with a flesh wound, the hated White man who stood behind him, whom you could not otherwise reach.

Robert Lewis Dabney (1820-1898) was, with James Henley Thornwell, one of the two most influential Old School Southern Presbyterian theologians. Descended from the famous French Huguenot D'Aubigné family, he inherited a keen intellect and a staunch commitment to the historic Calvinist faith. At the young age of seventeen, he graduated from Hampton-Sidney College in Virginia with a Bachelor of Arts degree, went on to earn a Master's degree from Virginia University five years later, and graduated from Union Theological Seminary in 1846. He served as a missionary in Louisa County, Virginia from 1846 to 1847, and pastored Tinkling Springs Presbyterian Church in Augusta County from 1847 to 1853. His designs for the Tinkling Springs church building and two others are credited for influencing church architecture in Virginia. He worked as Professor of Ecclesiastical History and Adjunct Professor of Systematic Theology at Union Theological Seminary between the years 1853 to 1869. He was a prolific writer, penning more than ten volumes of theological and other subject matter, including a biography of General Thomas Jonathan (Stonewall) Jackson. Dabney is perhaps best known for his service as chief of staff to General Jackson in the Confederate Army during the Valley Campaign of the War Between the States. He also was chaplain to the 18th Virginia Infantry. Near the end of his life, he served as moderator of the Presbyterian Church in the United States (from which the PCA of today is a direct descendent) and assisted in the foundation of what would later become the Austin Presbyterian Theological Seminary in Texas.

PART TWO:
TWENTIETH CENTURY

VIII

Race Relations – Whither?
by Lamuel Nelson Bell

We in the South have a race problem and we should face it squarely. The discriminations and injustices practiced against the Negroes are real and they need our attention. Equal opportunities for education and gainful employment should be theirs. Where deserved, we should not hesitate to accord them the respectful title of "Mister," "Mistress" or "Miss." Fairness should characterize all of our dealings with them.

But, as we hear some of the inflammatory and inaccurate propagandists for the colored people, and study what some in the Church evidently have as their aim in "Race Relations," we are alarmed and even dismayed.

In its "Annual Race Relations Message," the Federal Council has issued a statement as to what the Christian's attitude should be regarding race relations. This writer yields to no one on this question and would challenge any to have a more sincere desire for Christian spirit towards peoples of other races. This is not prideful boasting but comes from many years of actual experience in such relations and the knowledge of the mutual love and respect which now exists.

In reading this message from the Federal Council, one agrees heartily with those recommendations looking toward the elimination of unfair and unjust discriminations. But one looks in vain for any recognition of the fact that there is a line which must not be crossed. In fact this message states that Christians "should be unprejudiced and wise enough to bridge and cross the chasms of racial isolation and segregation."

Is racial segregation un-Christian? Is one un-Christian who feels that unrestricted social relations are unwise? If the Federal Council and those who accept the leadership of the Council in this matter take this position, we can but feel that harm must inevitably result. If, on the other hand, they will make a clear statement affirming that their goal is not unrestricted social equality, their leadership will not be regarded with distrust.

As we stated above; there is a line which must be drawn and which must not be crossed. This line was, we believe, established by God when He made men of different races. While Paul stated in his sermon on Mars' Hill, "God... hath made of one blood all nations of men for to dwell on all the face of the earth," he goes on and specifically states that God also determined "the bounds of their habitation."

We wish to affirm that we do not believe that segregation is un-Christian. In fact, it is a kindness to those of both races. If that one point is accepted by White and Negro leaders who are looking for a solution, a long step forward will have been taken.

This is not an abstract problem. Recently, the wife of an army officer was visiting her husband, a patient in a large military hospital. As she left his room and walked down the hospital corridor, she was stopped by a Negro soldier with the request for a "date" that evening. Such incidents will increase and now is the time for those who are genuinely concerned to see that all attempts to cross this line be stopped. If not, only sorrow and even worse discriminations lie ahead.

In our own Church we feel unwise things have been done. We cannot see that ultimate good can come from bringing Negro boys and girls to our Young People's Conferences. The attempt at the last Assembly to increasingly bring Negroes into the various conferences of our Church seemed, to the writer, an unkindness, rather than a kindness to our colored brethren.

This line which is fixed is racial. Why God saw fit to make some men White and some Black may go back to Genesis 9. Racial difference is a fact which no human philosophy can change.

This line is also biological. Cross the line and half-breeds result. Those of us who have lived for years in the Orient have seen the unhappiness, even agony, which has come from breaking over the barrier God has established.

Thank God, this line does not in any way affect the solution of the soul's need of the individual. Christ died for all and His salvation is free to all. The souls of every man, woman and child, be he Black, White, Yellow or Brown, are equally precious in God's sight. In fact, we insist that our Christian colored friends are our brothers in Christ and have a like precious hope and heritage, while those who are White but who deny the Lord Jesus Christ, are sons of God only by creation, and are not our brothers in Christ, but children of the devil, as Christ so plainly taught. Because of this, it is gratuitous in the extreme for the Federal Council to infer, as it does in the last paragraph of its "message," that "full fellowship in Christ at the foot of the Cross" is denied our colored brethren by those who insist on the maintenance of the God-ordained racial line in social relations.

God knows that we deplore present racial discriminations and injustices. Most of these, we believe, grow up and thrive in non-Christian circles. Leaders of recent race riots have been godless men of the lower social strata who have no Christian background.

Let those who talk so much about race relations recognize and hold valid this fundamental basis from which alone a satisfactory solution can come. If they refuse to acknowledge that such a division exists, they are but adding to the difficulties we face.

Lamuel Nelson Bell (1894-1973) was a medical missionary in China and father-in-law of evangelist, Billy Graham. He founded *The Southern Presbyterian Journal* in 1942, and later worked with Graham to found what later would become *Christianity Today*.

This editorial appeared in *The Southern Presbyterian Journal* (March 1944), Vol. II, No. 11.

IX

Dr. Benjamin M. Palmer
On Racial Barriers
by B. W. Crouch

Among the profound thinkers of a former generation was Dr. Benjamin M. Palmer, for several years the minister of the First Presbyterian Church in Columbia, S. C., and later of the First Church in New Orleans, La.

As a thinker as well as an orator, he had few peers – whether in the pulpit or on the platform, he always drew immense audiences and with his gracious gifts he swept them along with him. Dr. Palmer knew much of the Old South and slavery. He suffered as all Southerners the hardships of the War Between the States. He went through the days of Reconstruction with all its venality, corruption and horrors. He knew the Negro both as a slave and as a freeman. For them he had a tender regard and was always kind and helpful to them.

He recognized the fact that two races of men must live on the same soil and that each had a mission in God's economy.

But unlike the social uplifters and fanatics of today,

many in the North and some of their imitators in the South,
he was firmly convinced that the two races must be separate and free from social intermingling, and neither allowed to cross the bounds set both as taught by history
and in God's Word.

Unlike the Stanley Joneses and some of his cheap imitators – though Southern born and occupying places of
leadership in some Southern churches and preaching what
they call a "Social Gospel," meaning "all racial barriers
down" – Dr. Palmer held that these "racial barriers" were
erected by God Himself, and woe unto both races if they
are ever pulled down!

In an address he delivered to the graduating class in
1872 at Washington and Lee University, among other problems Dr. Palmer discussed so wisely and eloquently, was
the problem of race. In regard to this he said:

> Before all others, is the problem of race. So far as
> I can understand the teachings of history, there is one
> underlying principle which must control the question.
> It is indispensable that the purity of race shall be pre-
> served on either side; for it is the condition of life to
> the one, as to the other.
>
> The argument of this I base upon the declared
> policy of the Divine Administration from the days of
> Noah until now.

The speaker then tells of how and why language was
confounded and the people scattered abroad upon the face
of the earth. Then proceeding he says:

> Among the methods of fixed separation between
> these original groups, was the discrimination effected

by certain physical characteristics, so early introduced that no records of tradition or of stone assign their commencement; and so broadly marked that a class of physiologists deny the unity of human origin....

I certainly hold to the inspired testimony that "God hath made of one blood all nations of men for to dwell on the face of the earth." But there is no escape from the corresponding testimony, biblical and historical, that the human family, originally one, has been divided into certain large groups for the purpose of being kept historically distinct. And all attempts, in every age of the world, and from whatever motives, whether of ambitious dominion or of an infidel humanitarianism, to force these together, are identical in aim and parallel in guilt with the first usurpation and insurrection of the first Nimrod.

After citing instances of the ruin of Nations from a commixture of diverse races he continued:

The true policy of both races [meaning the Whites and the Negroes] is that they shall stand apart in their own social grade, in their own schools, in their own ecclesiastical organizations, under their own teachers and guides; but with all the kindness and helpful cooperation to which the old relations between the races and their present dependence on each other would naturally predispose.

I have said to the representatives of the Black race, as I have had opportunity, you gain nothing by a parasitic clinging to the White race; and immeasurably less, by trying to jostle them out of place.... Were I, a Black man, I should plead for a pure Black race, as, being a White man, I claim it for the White race; and should only ask the opportunity for it to work out its mission.

How different and sensible is the philosophy of this great divine, from the cheap and fanatical and foolish preachments of the Stanley Joneses and his few imitators occupying some Southern pulpits of today, who are endeavoring to pull down all the barriers between the races – barriers set by the Almighty Himself when He not only "made of one blood all nations of men for to dwell on the face of the earth," but also "set their bounds." If they would but know the truth: their advocacy of "social equality" under the guise of a social gospel, instead of removing "racial barriers," is calculated to bring about a race hatred that will issue in the destruction of all those kindly sentiments that the best type of Southern Whites have always, and even now, entertain for the Black man.

If the "social uplifters" of the North and their fanatical imitators in the South would find something else to do other than imagining they can change all history and improve on the Almighty's plan for the races, they would render a far greater service to the Black man of the South than in their foolish efforts as now proclaimed by them!

B.W. Crouch was a layman in the Presbyterian Church in the United States residing in Saluda, South Carolina. Originally a Methodist, he transferred to the PCUS and was a staunch opponent of a reunion between the Southern and Northern Presbyterian Churches.

This article appeared in *The Southern Presbyterian Journal*, Dec. 6, 1946, Vol. V, No. 12.

X

Non-Segregation Means
Eventual Intermarriage
by Rev. J. David Simpson

First, may I say that I have always been a friend of the Negro, and one vitally interested in his progress spiritually, intellectually, physically, and socially? I have not only thought and contended for his best interests, but I have constantly worked for his full advancement in every phase of life. I have, also, learned that the best friends of the Negro by and large are the Southern White people of high principle, who know the Negro better than any people in any other section of these United States, in spite of contentions to the contrary.

By way of introduction, I will say further, that I am positively convinced that such problems as may come up in the South between the Negro and White races will be solved to the full satisfaction of all concerned if the South is left alone to solve them without outside interference and pressure groups. The Negro in the South does not interpret the racial propaganda from other sections of our nation to be contributory and helpful to his uplift, but instead, has been filled with fear and suspicion of his good Southern White friends because of the misleading nature of much of this propaganda. The Negro in the South has actually become frantic with the wildest of imaginations coursing through his frame, that all of this "much-ado" about his condition would not be going on, if some uprising against him were not in the making. Racial propagandists and agitators are actually doing both the Negro and White man an irreparable harm in the South.

Coming to the question of non-segregation, it is my conviction after close observation that non-segregation is not desired by the well-meaning, intelligent, racially pure Negro. The Negro does not want White people in his church, school, fraternity, or any of his social institutions. He does not seek social intermingling of the races, as he is fully aware of the dire consequences and dangers even if the White man wanted such social intermingling. One of these dangers is that of intermarriage, and in spite of every argument to the contrary, it will surely come to pass if free social intermingling between the races displaces segregation over the whole of our nation. There is an affinity, the like of which many people are strangely unaware, between the Negroes and Whites. Especially, is this true in the South where Negroes have been thrown closer with White people and greater numbers of Negroes reside. Racial barriers and distinctive characteristics of race and color will eventually break down and no longer prove to be stumbling blocks preventing marriage, if non-segregation comes in and continues over a period of time. Our children and children's children will be called upon to endure a cross and burden the like of which none of us in our time have had to endure. The cross and burden will be that of resisting and repelling every natural urge of affection ripening into the desire for marriage between the Negro and White as the years go by. True it is that some of this attraction may in the beginning be of a sensual or sexual nature, resulting in immorality or marriage on a sensual love basis, but this does not by any means guarantee that the true love of sentiment and pure affection, on a very high plane, would not also be the experience between the opposite sexes of many Negroes and Whites. Even Platonic love, or every proven form of attraction, such as has resulted in marriage between the members of one race, could conceivably be present, and in fact, is present between the members of different races thrown together. Is this not proving true between Mongolians and Whites right before our eyes today?

It has been said that Negresses of an immoral character are ambitious to have their offspring begotten or fathered by White men in order to infuse all the White blood they can into their race, thereby hoping to get better standing in society through the Mulatto strain. If this is true, then it is a lasting shame on us that Negroes should seem to seek advancement in such a shameful and sinful manner. I reiterate, the true well-meaning, intelligent thinking Negro wants segregation continued without free social intermingling of the two races. He knows the dangers ahead, and he further knows that he can advance in his own institutions without the presence of the White race under a much healthier status educationally, spiritually, physically, and morally, provided his institutions are properly supported. He knows definitely of the terrific consequences upon the social order of an increasing hybrid race. The Mulatto strain brings stultification of progress, the gradual fading of the genius strain, and the slow deterioration and moral degeneracy of the social order.

The society for the advancement of the Negro race in America says that we are now losing 12,000 Negroes annually to the White race. They are being absorbed in the White race, and we know that they would not be in such position as to pass for Whites and be absorbed if it were not for such intermarriage as may already exist or practices of immorality between the two races.

If you are in doubt as to the truth of what has been written thus far, take a cue from the words recently uttered by the Rev. John Bodo, pastor of the Wolff Memorial Presbyterian Church of Newark, N.J. In speaking of the race question, Dr. Bodo says: "My daughter will marry whomsoever she chooses. The only reason I might discourage her from marrying a Negro is my fear of the punishment her White friends – even the most 'tolerant' ones – would inflict on her for doing it."

Lastly, I want to express my further conviction that the Scriptures teach segregation, and most positively do not teach the pattern of non-segregation that is being so strongly urged upon the South by pressure groups and agitators from the outside. Acts 17:26 says: "And hath made of one blood all nations of men for to dwell on all the face of the earth, and hath determined the times before appointed, and the bounds of their habitation." This verse, by some of our leading biblical commentators and theologians, is used over and over again in defense of segregation of the races, and to their interpretation I agree.

The fact is, that the latter part of the verse teaches just the opposite of non-segregation and free social intermingling. The determined bounds of all races or nations as it is used here in this verse, being established of God, seems definitely to teach the racial boundary line for all races and their integrity kept inviolate. This applies to all races – Yellow, Brown, Red, Black, and White. They should have segregated life and social intermingling to themselves to preserve the true and pure strain of their respective races.

True it is that all nations are of one blood, as is proven by the typing of blood plasma which transcends the races and can be used freely on any race as well as within the confines of the particular race from which it was taken, thus proving the "one blood" teaching of the Scriptures. It is true, also, that all races are capable of producing an hybrid or mixed race through marriage between them, showing or proving the "one blood" statement of the Scriptures to be true. Yet, the "bounds of their habitation," which follows "made of one blood," leaves us, it seems, in no doubt that God did not want the racial bounds separating the races broken down into hybrid races, which will most certainly eventuate if all races move in and out among themselves with non-segregation and free social intermingling. The amalgamation of races is definitely unscriptural. The integrity and pure strain of all races should be preserved inviolate, with segregation as a necessity, if this verse of God's Holy Word is to be fully observed and applied in its true meaning to the social fabric of the world.

Take a look at the South American mixture of races and see if you think God's approval and blessing has been upon it. Observe their physical and social structure, their progress, their initiative, their ingenuity, and general out-look upon life, and see if you think God's approval and blessing has been upon it. Then turn and compare their civilization with that of the pure strain of one race or many races kept inviolate as to mixture, where Christian enlight-enment has gone – social, educational, physical, moral – and what have you? What do you think the "Tower of Ba-bel" confusion story in the Scriptures meant if it did not mean that even the races should, for the most part, estab-lish even their territorial boundary lines for their habita-tion, as well as racial? Yes, I repeat, non-segregation of the races is to my mind unscriptural; whereas, segregation of the races is to my mind definitely scriptural. Marriage be-tween sharp racial lines of color and characteristics such as is found in the Red, Brown, Black, White and Yellow races is unscriptural; marriage within the confines of separate races is definitely scriptural, and is enjoined upon the social order. Amalgamation, miscegenation and hybrid races are unscriptural; races kept inviolate as to mixture, preserved pure in strain and their integrity kept, is positively taught in the Scriptures. I repeat again, non-segregation means eventual intermarriage. We usually marry the people with whom we freely associate. "And (God) hath made of one blood all nations of men for to dwell on all the face of the earth, and hath determined the times before appointed, and the bounds of their habitation."

⚮

J. David Simpson was a PCUS minister from Aberdeen, Mississippi. This article appeared in *The South-ern Presbyterian Journal*, March 15, 1948, Vol. VI, No. 22.

XI

The Interracial Brotherhood Movement: Is It Scriptural?
by Dr. Walter A. Plecker, M.D.

Three times in the early history of the human family man sinned universally. Three times sin called forth the wrath of God.

1. Adam sinned, and was driven from Eden, Gen. 3:24: "So he drove out the man; and he placed at the east of the garden of Eden cherubim, and a flaming sword which turned every way, to keep the way of the tree of life."

2. The sons of God took them wives of the daughters of men, Gen. 6:2. "And God looked upon the earth and behold, it was corrupt; for all flesh had corrupted his way upon the earth." v 12. Then came the flood.

3. "And the whole earth was of one language, and of one speech." Gen. 11:1: "And they said, Go to, let us build us a city, and a tower, whose top may reach unto heaven; and let us make us a name lest we be scattered abroad upon the face of the whole earth. And the Lord came down to see the city and the tower, which the children of men builded." v 4-5. "And the Lord said, Go to, let us go down,

and there confound their language, that they may not understand one another's speech." v 6-7. Then came the third
great stroke of God's wrath upon pride-filled man. "So the
Lord scattered them abroad from thence upon the face of
all the earth." v 8.

Ham had earlier made sport of his father Noah, whom
he found naked under the influence of wine. He told his
brothers Shem and Japheth, who in filial loyalty, "covered
the nakedness of their father."

"And Noah awoke from his wine, and knew what his
younger son had done unto him." v 24.

Noah in righteous indignation, knowing the lower
moral and, probably, mental character of Ham, either with
divine approval, or of his own intuition, said: "Cursed be
Canaan; a servant of servants shall he be unto his brethren." v 25.

Noah then blessed his two loyal sons, and with each
blessing repeated the curse poured forth upon Ham in the
name of his son Canaan – "and Canaan shall be his servant." v 26-27. How truly has that prophesy been fulfilled
during more than forty centuries since its utterance.

Let us now consider further the cause and result of the
happenings at Babel.

Following the creation of man, male and female, God
commanded: "Be fruitful and multiply, and replenish the
earth, and subdue it." Gen. 1:28. This command was repeated to Noah after the flood. Gen. 9:1 and 7. Under the
leadership, probably, of Nimrod, grandson of Ham, who
"began to be a mighty one in the earth," Gen. 11:8, the people gave as their reason for building the tower, "Lest we be
scattered upon the face of the whole earth."

The attempt to avoid "replenishing the earth" was as contrary to the will of God, as was Adam's sin in eating the forbidden fruit, or the sin of the antediluvian descendants of Seth, who took wives from the offspring of godless Cain, or other godless children of Adam.

The punishment for this third universal sin of the human race was quicker, but just as positive, as the punishment for the first and second sins involving mankind.

Instead of destructive punishment, God inflicted one which would be in conformity with His will previously declared, and which would force man, willing or unwilling, to carry out His divine purpose that the world be peopled with man of different and clearly marked races, occupying lands as far apart as was geographically possible.

Descendants of Japheth were directed to Europe and they subdivided into distinct types – the light haired, long-headed Nordics of northern Europe, the broad-faced Alpines of central Europe and the dark-haired Mediterranean type of south Europe.

The children of Shem were likewise divided into types from the White Jewish to the Mongolian Chinese.

When it came to the children of Ham, Noah's prediction that they should be of such a marked and distinct type as to everywhere and at all times, set them off as a race to themselves, servants of their brethren, seems to have been in line with God's plan and when they were headed for Africa, they had, as we may well believe, not only the marks of distinctive speech, but of physical characteristics also.

Science finds nowhere an explanation for the Black skin, curly hair, flat thick features, and widely differing mental, and after thirty-four years of study of racial mixture and characteristics, as Virginia Registrar of Vital Statistics, I may safely say, of moral characteristics also.

The only explanation is found in God's miraculous change of Noah's descendants into family language groups. What hindered God from giving the descendants of Ham the marked physical changes of color and features, with mental and moral difference as we find them today, all in keeping with Noah's prophecy, or curse, as being the servant of all?

The Federal Council of Churches, and some of our own and other denominations are now making forced social fellowship, rather than belief in salvation through Christ, the standards of Christianity, with the intermarriage of Whites and full-blooded Negroes legal in eighteen States and the District of Columbia and the intermarriage of Whites and mixed bloods of varying degrees of admixture legal in nineteen others. That, with closer social and physical contact, is the specter looming up before us, together with an increasing number of extra-marital mixed births.

Is any action tending to the furthering of this end justified in the face of God's decisive action in the separation of races at Babel?

Read the graphic account in the last chapter of Ezra of how Ezra forced the many Jewish men who had taken Canaanitish wives to separate from, and return them to their former homes, together with their children. Because of the great number of the guilty, and because of much rain, they begged that some time be given them for the great task.

Many seem to have evaded Ezra's demand, for twenty-three years after, Nehemiah faced the same problem, Neh. 13:23-31. He said, 13:25: "I contended with them and cursed them, and smote certain of them, and plucked off their hair, and made them swear by God, saying, ye shall not give your daughters unto their sons, nor take their daughters unto your sons, or for yourselves." That was far from the social or religious intercourse advocated so vigorously today with the Black children of Ham living amongst us. It is unnatural. It means race destruction. It is contrary to the teaching of God's Word. The true Negro knows that it is not natural; he does not desire it, and is making no effort to bring that about. It is the Mulattoes who make the stir for racial unity. The true Negroes are much happier and better satisfied in developing their own varying culture as they have always contentedly done.

We should however extend them the hand of Christian fellowship and render all aid possible in teaching and guiding them along right lines. That need not involve social contact with social intermarriage, with the mixed breeds as the end results.

Even within our own race, types of society and culture based upon heritage education, and mode of living, separate almost as clearly as does race itself.

It should not be considered a crime or unchristian when an educated and highly cultured person and one entirely the opposite cannot associate together upon terms of social intimacy. The same is true, if they almost unconsciously and without studied purpose find themselves even in churches, separating into homogenous groups. In cities, the place of residence is largely the determining factor.

About the only text quoted for the strained "interracial

brotherhood movement" being worked up with a great flare, is Acts 17:26: "And hath made of one blood all nations of men to dwell on all the face of the earth." Note that they are to dwell – not dwell together – on *all* the face of the earth. When the latter part of the verse is read: "and hath determined the bounds of their habitation," we see clearly that God's purpose is exactly the opposite to close interracial contact. To prevent that very thing, God at Babel gave them a distinct language, extreme physical differences, and sent them to the most remote parts of the earth. Noah certainly did not place his three sons upon a plane of equality – one was emphatically in a lower class, and so has history shown that Ham's descendants have been. God in the physical, and other changes wrought in Ham's descendants, shows plainly the correctness of Noah's judgment.

What has been said applies to but little over half of the colored population of our country – the pure descendants of African stock.

The other half – mixed breeds – shun the pure blood Negroes, and are interested only in securing classification as a part of the White race. Their thought of "fellowship" places that one idea uppermost from first to last.

Find any, if you can, of the near-Whites who are interested in "Christian fellowship" and that alone. Their first and only thought is crossing the social line. The discussion of that subject from its many angles, and final result, will require the writing of a volume.

Why should our Church be led by the Federal Council of Churches to strive for close social contact and intimacy, directly contrary to the will of God as pointed out above?

"Interracial Brotherhood" will not correct the overwhelming error of our forefathers in admitting to our shore Black men assigned by God to Africa as the "bounds of their habitation."

⊷

Walter Ashby Plecker (1861-1947) was the son of a returned Confederate veteran, and a physician and public health advocate in Richmond, Virginia. He served as first registrar of Virginia's Bureau of Vital Statistics and drafted and lobbied for the State's Racial Integrity Act of 1924. He was a devout member of the PCUS, and helped to establish churches throughout Virginia.

This essay appeared in *The Southern Presbyterian Journal,* Jan. 1947, Vol. V, No. 17.

XII

The Social Separation of the Races
by Rev. Wm. H. Frazer, D.D. Litt.D., LL.D.

There is much agitation now being made and action taken in regard to "equal rights" of the Negroes, especially those in the South. I yield to no man in my desire to see every human being receive his "rights," and I have no apology to make as to my record in the matter of granting them. However, much that is being said, and done, is going to go beyond the limits which are being sought.

That there should be a guarantee of the rights of every one is a self-evident proposition in a democratic country. That the Negro has been deprived of some of his rights is a fact that cannot be overlooked or gainsaid. However, the securing of his rights is one thing, and the consequence of the present trend of agitation, and constitutional interpretation, is quite another. To say that he should have equal rights politically, economically, educationally, ecclesiastically, and otherwise is but to repeat a position that has been contended for by many of our Southern citizens for generations.

But to say that the drawing of a line of demarcation between the races as to their mingling together in society, in schools, in churches, and eating places and hotels constitutes a denial of this right is quite a different matter. The so-called "segregation" practice is no more a casting of a slur at the Negro than it is at the White race. It is simply a racial separation in order to protect the interests of both races, and to preserve the racial integrity of both races.

There should be as much respect paid to the Negro race in its circle as there is to the White race in its circle. Christian courtesy is not violated by assigning each race to its own circle in these matters.

The awful consequences attending and following the breaking down of this separating barrier must be considered in the interest of both races.

I. We believe in the "social separation" of the races because we think that God believes in it. Racial purity was of prime importance to Him when He brought Israel out of Egypt and settled them in the land of Canaan. He forbade the intermarriage with the people who were already in the land. (Read Deut. 7:3, Joshua 23:12-13). And when Ezra returned to set up the worship of the restored temple, one of the first things that he did was to purge the people of "mixed marriages." (Ezra 10:3, 10, 11).

II. We believe in the "social separation" of the races because we think that God not only believed in it, but that He commanded it. The above passages are evidence of this fact. The oft-quoted passage from Acts 17:26 has been discounted, and even sneered at. However, to me it still has a meaning. Paul is declaring the common origin of mankind, and equally as emphatic is he declaring the differentiation of mankind. Environment does many things but it does not change "leopard spots," nor does it erase racial lines.

III. We believe in the "social separation" of the races because of the things to which the "mixing" of the races leads.

1. It leads inevitably to miscegenation. One thing that is apparent from the history of social economy is the fact that whenever you erase the separating lines and allow a free social intercourse, it results in miscegenation. There is bound to come about "attraction" among the races that will result in scandal and shame. No opposite sexes can mingle together freely without this consequence. Any student of social economy knows this to be a fact of history.

2. It will lead, indirectly, to confusion, strife, hatred and bloodshed. Many people will resent the extent to which it will inevitably go and will resist it.

3. Miscegenation will lead to a weakening of the resistance to certain diseases by the hybrid offspring. Dr. S. F. Hoffman, one of the outstanding statisticians of America in his time, the officer of the New York Life Insurance Company in that capacity, made many tests of this matter, and finally announced in his famous report on "The Race Traits and Tendencies of the American Negro" that he found that scrofula and pulmonary diseases were less easily resisted by the Mulatto than by the one with either pure African or Caucasian blood.

4. Miscegenation, which is the inevitable consequence of non-separation, will reduce the American citizen to a "common denominator." You will put back the race which has imbibed the spirit and adapted itself to the progress of hundreds of generations of civilization and culture, to ac-

commodate the pace of the backward race of only a comparatively few generations of civilization and culture. It would be like placing a senior in college in the same class with a student in grammar school. It would be like adapting the stride of a grown man to the step of a child!

We should respect the rights of the Negro; his right to live in his own society, worship in his own churches, educate his children in his own schools, travel in his own compartments, and lodge in his own hotels. And when we do give him this right and the whole-hearted respect that should go along with it, and ask that he give the White man the same right and accord him the same respect, we will have Jesus' view of the relation of races, as our example and guide. He did not try to merge the Samaritans and the Jews. He accorded the Samaritans all due respect, gave to them His ministering service, and suggested in one of His parables the humanitarian conduct which they exemplified.

∽∞∾

William Henry Frazer (1873-1953) was a native of Lafayette, Alabama. He graduated with a Bachelor of Arts degree from Southwestern Presbyterian University in Clarksville, Tennessee in 1897 and went on to earn a Bachelor of Divinity degree from Union Theological Seminary in New York in 1899, a Doctor of Divinity degree from the Presbyterian College at Clinton, South Carolina in 1909, a Doctor of Literature degree from Davidson College in North Carolina in 1929, and a Doctor of Laws from Southwestern University at Memphis, Tennessee in 1937. Ordained to the Presbyterian ministry in 1899, he pastored churches in the cities of Atlanta and Macon, Georgia, Clinton and Anderson, South Carolina, and Charlotte, North Carolina. He also served as president of Queens Chicora College (now Queens University) in Charlotte. He authored several books and essays, including *Bible Notes For Bible Students* and "The Afro-American: His Past, Present and Future."

This essay appeared in *The Southern Presbyterian Journal,* July 15, 1950, Vol. IX, No. 6.

XIII

Is Segregation Unchristian?
by Rev. J. E. Flow, D.D.

In *The Presbyterian Outlook* of July 30, there are two letters to the editor from young people who very ardently advocate non-segregation in our churches. They claim that segregation is unchristian, and they describe as cowards, and brand as "hypocrites," those who do not agree with them.

I believe in segregation and am not at all disturbed by anything they may call me and others who share my views. I attribute their "zeal without knowledge" to the exuberance of youth and to their being furnished for light housekeeping in the upper story.

Segregation was decreed by God Himself in one historical instance. God called Abram out of Ur of the Chaldees, to go into a land which he should afterwards receive as an inheritance. The Patriarchs Abraham, Isaac, and Jacob lived in that land for many years. Jacob's clan, because of famine, went down into Egypt, and were settled in the land of Goshen, where they remained 400 years. Then God sent Moses to lead the tribes of Israel out of Egypt into the wilderness for 40 years, and Joshua led them into the land of Canaan, where the various tribes were settled. For fifteen hundred years till the birth of Christ they were a segregated nation. They were forbidden by God to mingle socially, to intermarry, or to amalgamate with the nations around them. They did not always obey God, but nevertheless God commanded it and many times punished them when they disobeyed His command. If allowed to mingle socially with each other, the inevitable result would be amalgamation, either with or without marriage.

Out of that segregated nation, through inspired prophets from time to time, from Moses to Malachi, came the revealed will of God in the Old Testament. Out of that segregated nation, came the Saviour of the world, and the New Testament which tells us of Him. Does anyone dare to say that God made a mistake in segregating the Jewish nation? Does anyone dare to say that segregation is wrong and un-Christian when the Almighty Himself did it? The only God we know, or care to know, is the God revealed in the Scriptures, and He never makes a mistake and never does wrong. "He is glorious in holiness, fearful in praises doing wonders."

I believe in segregation for three reasons:

1. In the first place, I believe that segregation is in harmony with the plan and purpose of the Almighty Himself, as the best means to prevent amalgamation of the races. He used it in the case of His chosen people Israel.

Let us face some stubborn facts: We have three most distinct races of men distinguished by the color of their faces – the Yellow man, the Black man, and the White man. Who made one man's face yellow, one black, and another white? That question is not hard to answer, for there is only one Being in the universe that could do such a thing, and He is the Almighty, the Creator of all things. But why did He do it? He has not told us except in general terms. In Rev. 4:11 we read: "The four and twenty elders fall down before Him that sat on the throne, and worship him that liveth forever and ever and cast their crowns before the throne, saying, Thou art worthy, O Lord, to receive glory and honor, and power; For thou hast created all things, and for thy pleasure they are and were created." The only reason we are given is that it pleased God. In the early creation of the world we are told, "He spake and it was done. He commanded and it stood fast."

But when and where did this change take place? It must have been after the days of Noah and the flood. When the people began to build the tower of Babel, in the land of Shinar, God interfered and confused their language so that they could no longer understand each other's speech and were forced to scatter out in different directions. They spoke at least three different languages – maybe more, but at least three. The descendants of Shem, the oldest son of Noah, moved eastward and remained on the continent of Asia. The descendants of Ham went west to the land of Canaan, then south into the continent of Africa. The descendants of Japheth moved north and went overland through the Caucasus mountains, between the Black and the Caspian seas and inhabited the continent of Europe, and became known as the Caucasian, or White race.

Sometime in the centuries that followed, the Yellow man was found in China, the Black man in Africa, and the

White man in Europe. Paul said to the Athenians: "God hath made of one blood all nations of men, for to dwell on all the face of the earth, and hath determined the times before appointed, and the bounds of their habitation." Our God, the God of all wisdom, has never admitted that He ever made a mistake, in this or in any other instance. And He certainly has not authorized any men to correct His "mistake," or to improve upon His plan. In Latin America they tried to improve on God's plan, but did they? The Spanish and Portugese conquerors amalgamated freely with the native Indians, then they imported Negro slaves from Africa, and became amalgamated with them, so there is no color line and no segregation south of the Rio Grande. But do they have a higher stage of Christian civilization than the people of the U.S. and Canada? How does their missionary zeal in foreign lands compare with ours? I would advise all those who can't stand segregation, to go to the Rio Grande River and buy a one way ticket and they will never be troubled any more with it. God made one man's face yellow, another black, and another white because it pleased Him to do so and he means for them to remain that way. It is presumptuous for any man to think that he can improve on God's plan.

2. In the second place I believe in segregation because, it is not only in the plan of God, but it is in harmony with a well known law of nature, stated in the proverb, "Bird's of a feather will flock together." Sparrows will not flock with robins, neither will ducks migrate with geese.

The Chinaman feels happier and more at liberty with his own people in his own churches, schools, and communities than he does mingling with other people whose tastes and habits are different from his. The Negro, if let alone by these ceaseless agitators, feels more at home and happier among his own people in church, school, and communities than to be forced to mingle with other people who are not always congenial. I want the Negro to have as good school buildings and equipment as the White people have. But I will say that there is not a school house in this country, White or colored, that is not a far better house with far better equipment than I had sixty-five years ago. And with God's blessing, I got an education.

I want to see the Negro live in good houses where he can be comfortable and self respecting. O, but they are poor, they say! Yes, but poverty is not confined to one race – there are many poor White people who have a hard time. As long as we have wars there will always be poverty and plenty of it.

3. In the third place I believe in race segregation because it contributes to the harmony and peace among the races. The Christian White man does not hate the Negro, but wants to help him in an understanding way, and does do it. The Christian Negro does not hate the White man, but respects and honors the Christian White man as his best friend and is appreciative for any kindness that comes his way.

It is the wicked White man and the wicked Negro that hate each other and are ready to fly at each other's throats on little provocation. This is one reason why the Christian White man in the South wants race segregation – for the protection of the Negro. There never was a race riot that the Negro did not get the worst of it. We do not like race riots nor any other form of murder. We like to have peace and good will among the races who are compelled to live together in the same land. This condition is not limited to the South, as some people with very short memories would have us believe, for there have been many more race riots in the North than have been in the South. The slums of the Northern cities are worse than anything we have in the South.

I am advocating segregation not as a perfect solution of the vexatious race problem, but only as a help. We do not meet with perfect solutions in this imperfect world. But as Christians we should be kind and helpful to all men. There is no occasion for pride in the study of this difficult question.

Paul in writing to the Corinthians, 1 Cor. 4:11, "For who maketh thee to differ from another? And what hast thou that thou didst not receive? And if thou didst receive it, why dost thou glory as if thou didst not receive it?" You and I had no choice as to the color of our faces or the land of our birth. This ought to make all of us humble and thankful to God, and very charitable and kind to our fellow men.

There will be no segregation in Heaven for there will be no sin, nor danger of race riots there. We will all speak the same language, sing the same song, be clothed in the same white robes, and worship the same God who sits on the Great White Throne, and we will all be of the same color – the color that Elijah and Moses had on the Mount of Transfiguration with Christ.

❧

J. E. Flow was a minister in the PCUS and pastored churches in Alderson, West Virginia and Concord, North

Carolina. He also served as Stated Clerk and Treasury of the Upper Missouri Presbytery.

This article appeared in *The Southern Presbyterian Journal*, Aug. 29, 1951, Vol. X, No. 18.

XIII

Brotherhood and Race
by Dr. Morton H. Smith, Th.D.

1. Introduction

The Christian finds in the Bible an infallible rule of faith and of practice. This means that as the Christian is faced with various problems of life he should look to the Bible to determine his belief and practice. The problem of race relations is no exception. Not the traditions of our fathers or the emotions that we may have, but the Bible is to be our one and only rule of life. It is for this reason that we shall seek to let the Bible speak for itself. We must be most careful in a situation such as this not to try and force the Bible into our own preconceived notions. After all, the Bible is to be heard, because it is the very Word of God.

There are genuine differences of opinion among true Bible believing Christians regarding what the Bible teaches about race relations. It might do well to indicate the basic views. A great many Christians feel that the only proper relations between the races is to be found in complete racial integration, including the privilege of intermarriage and the amalgamation of the races. On the other hand there are those who feel that certainly intermarriage is wrong, and that in order to prevent temptation to such, the practice of segregation should be enforced between the races, especially in social realms. Between these two groups are many who are not certain that there is a moral issue involved, and they favor either integration or segregation for various lesser reasons. Involved in each of the first two views is the condemnation of the other. The integrationist says that segregation is sinful and wrong, and the segregationist says the same of integration.

It is our purpose in this study to examine the various biblical grounds given by both groups to see just what the Bible does teach. Does it condemn segregation? Does it condemn integration? Does it insist on either of these cultural patterns?

II. The Unity of Mankind

As one studies the origin of man in the Bible it is evident that the Bible teaches that all men descend from one common pair of first parents. This is clearly set forth in the first chapters of Genesis, where the creation of Adam and Eve is presented. Not only do we find the unity of the race in the original creation, but again in the flood we find all of humanity destroyed except for one family, from whom all the peoples of the earth have come. This unity of human kind is further confirmed in the common nature that we all possess. It is seen in the fact that we are all sinners. It is seen in the fact that the Gospel is offered to all men alike.

The Apostle Paul affirms this unity in the Areopagus address recorded in Acts 17. He says, "And He made of one every nation of men to dwell on all the face of the earth...." (Acts 17:26). Paul in this sermon is addressing an audience of pagan philosophers. His main thrust is to the effect that though they indicate their basic skepticism and ignorance in worship, he comes to declare to them the Living and True God. Having spoken of Him as Creator of all things, which is the most basic distinction of the Christian Faith, he then points out the fact that all men are His creatures. And, even despite the differences of national and racial heritage among men, they are all one human kind, and thus should seek and worship the One Living and True God. No race or group, no matter how civilized or educated or cultured can get away from this fact. We are all the creatures of God, and thus we all should seek His glory as our chief end.

On the basis of this unity of mankind the integrationist teaches that we are all brothers, and should thus ignore all differences and mix as one race. There is a plea to forget racial and national differences and simply amalgamate into one common brotherhood. It should be noted, in passing, that the biblical concept of brotherhood is not primarily that of the physical unity, but rather that of the spiritual unity that Christians, who know God as Father through Jesus Christ, know and experience.

III. The Diversity of Mankind

It is rather striking to see that the very verse used by the integrationists as supporting their position also speaks of the diversity of peoples. The verse reads: "And He made of one every nation of men to dwell on all the face of the earth, having determined their appointed seasons, and the bounds of their habitation" (Acts 17:26). Notice that the verse not only teaches the fact of the basic unity of mankind, but also the fact of diversity of men into different nations and groups. In an earlier lesson we considered the origin of the nations, and we believe also of the races, in connection with the Tower of Babel. There in Genesis 11 we find the history of man's attempt to rebel against God's command to disperse and replenish the earth by remaining together as a unified people. There, we see that it is God Himself who scattered the people, enforcing this by the confusion of tongues. There we have the account of the origin of the various languages. This may not be the origin of the races, but it certainly is the Divine separation of peoples into different groups. It may well be that the origin of the races is to be found in Genesis 10 where we find the genealogies of the three sons of Noah. Many of the names of the descendants appear later as the names of tribes and peoples. For example, the sons of Ham were Cush, Mizraim, Put, and Canaan. These names became the names of various regions where these tribes lived. Cush is the ancient name of Ethiopia; Mizraim is the name of Egypt; Put denotes Libya of North Africa, and Canaan was the name of the land later to become Palestine. The descendants of Shem are still known as the Semitic people. Though it is not absolutely demonstrable that the modern races stem directly from these three divisions, it seems likely that the primitive origin of the races is to be seen here.

It is certain that in the combined accounts of the genealogies of the sons of Noah and the dispersion at the Tower of Babel we find God's direct action of separation of different elements of the human race into different groups. On the basis of this fact it would seem that the principle of separation of peoples or of segregation is not necessarily wrong *per se*. In fact it seems clearly to be God's order of things, in order to see that man fulfills his God-appointed tasks on earth.

IV. The Practice of Segregation in the Old Testament

As one traces the account of God's dealing with men through the Old Testament, this principle of the cutting off of a particular people from all the other peoples was used by God to preserve unto Himself a peculiar people. Abraham was called out from the other nations and peoples around him. His descendants failed to keep themselves separate from the people of Canaan, and thus God, in His all wise Providence, brought them down into Egypt, where they were set apart by the Egyptians in a segregated area. It should be noted that this segregation of Abraham's seed was done by God ultimately for the purpose of preserving their religious purity, yet it was done by means of racial segregation. This is not the situation that faces us today, but at least the principle of segregation is seen as something that is not inherently evil.

Following the Exodus the Israelites continued the policy of segregation. Moses clearly commanded against intermarriage with other peoples. See Deut. 7:3. Of course, this was a warning that had particular reference to the preservation of the people of God as a pure people racially, but more especially religiously. The first period of man's history which ended with the flood showed the tragic result of the intermarriage of the godly seed with the ungodly. This is clearly seen in Genesis 6. Ever since that time the marriage of God's people with the non-believer has been condemned. This remains true today, just as much as it was true in the days of Moses. Paul teaches that Christians ought not to be "unequally yoked together with unbelievers" (2 Cor. 6:14). This passage may apply to more than marriage, but it certainly applies to that relation.

Though the Israelites sinned and mixed with the pagans around them, they saw that it had contributed to their exile, and thus in Ezra 9 and 10 we find again the command against marriage with non-Israelites. This is repeated again by the last prophet of the Old Testament (Malachi 2:10-16). Again, this had the double aim of preserving a people as distinct, but particularly of preserving their religious purity.

V. The New Testament and Segregation

The question may be asked as to whether or not the New Testament sets this aside. With the coming of Jesus Christ and the completion of His work on earth we have the close of the period of particularity, in which God openly revealed Himself to only one nation. With the giving of the Great Commission we have the opening of a new period, namely that of universality. This is the period in which God offers His grace and mercy to the whole world. Ultimately the death of Judaism came with the death of Jesus Christ on the cross. And yet it was this very death of Christ that was to become the heart and core of the new form of the Gospel, which was to be proclaimed throughout the whole world. Pentecost saw the beginning of this new universalistic period of the Gospel, and it is not without significance that God, at Pentecost, answers the confusion of tongues at Babel with the gift of tongues to the Apostles, which could be understood by all people. This sign spoke of the universal offer of the Gospel to all peoples, and it may also have indicated the basic spiritual unity of all who accept the Gospel.

Paul is very clear about the fact that there is a basic unity of all in the Gospel. The Gentiles have been brought into the same Body as the Jews. (See Eph. 2:11-22; Gal. 3:28; Col. 3:11). Galatians 3:28 reads: "There can be neither Jew nor Greek, there can be neither bond nor free, there can be no male and female; for ye are all one man in Christ Jesus." Here Paul is setting forth the real unity that exists in the Church, and yet it can hardly be maintained that he meant to imply that there were no real and continued distinctions within the group that he lists. The Christian faith is not a religion that demands the erasure of all diversity between us. Rather there is in the Christian Faith a unity in diversity, and a diversity in unity. There may even be a reflection in the Church of the unity and diversity that exist within the Godhead. God is both One and Three. He is One God who exists in Three distinct Persons. The whole thrust of 1 Cor. 12 is that there is diversity within the Body of Christ, the Church. Even in spiritual matters within the Church the Apostle makes a distinction between men and women. Women are to keep silent in the Church. Throughout his epistles Paul makes distinctions and gives different exhortations to different groups within the Church. Thus Paul's doctrine of the unity of the Church should not be construed as teaching that the Church should forget or seek to erase the God-given distinctions, as some integrationists teach.

There are even to be found in Paul's writings a recognition of the continued differences that existed between Jewish and Gentile Christians. Some of the Jewish Christians continued in some of the Old Testament practices, such as Sabbath observance, worship in the Temple, etc. (Rom. 14:5-6; Acts 18:18; 21:23-29). Paul himself joined into certain Jewish forms on special occasions, becoming as a Jew to the Jews and as a Gentile to the Gentiles. Thus it is evident that the Apostle does not insist on a distinctionless mass of people within the Church, but rather recognizes individuals of great diversities.

Jesus, though He dealt primarily with Jews, did on occasion deal with non-Jewish people, such as the Samaritan woman and the Syro-phenician woman. He did not ignore their differences or necessarily seek to erase them. Though He ultimately gave them of His grace and mercy as He did to all who came to Him, He did deal differently with them. Thus He too exemplifies the principle of diversity in unity.

VI. Summation of Biblical Principles and Conclusion

If we were to summarize our findings in this biblical study, we would have to say first of all that the Bible does not condemn segregation.

On the other hand it does not necessarily condemn integration. This being the case this whole matter falls into the realm of Christian liberty. Where the Bible is not clear cut on a matter the individual Christian must decide the case on the basis of his own conscience before God. Paul in Romans 14 teaches further regarding Christian liberty that we must be most careful not to condemn a fellow Christian who may or may not feel as we do about some specific matter. How Christians of all areas of our country need to learn to follow those injunctions of the Apostle!

Having stated this as our basic conclusion we do need to add a general principle which may be derived more indirectly from Scripture. It has to do with the problem of intermarriage between the races. Is it right to mix the races with the aim of amalgamation? On the basis of the fact that God has made the different races as different races it would seem to be at least questionable as to whether man should seek to amalgamate the races. Babel was an attempt to do so. God showed His displeasure with this by scattering man, the effects of which we still have with us. Who are we to fly in the face of God's revealed will? Dr. B.M. Palmer, the first Moderator of our General Assembly, stated the case very effectively at Washington and Lee University in 1872:

> But so far as I can understand the teachings of history, there is one underlying principle which must control the question. It is indispensable that the purity of race be preserved on either side; for it is the condition of life to the one, as much as to the other.

This is certainly true. If God has made the different races to accomplish specific destinies, then they can only do so if they maintain their integrity as distinct races. To the Negro, Dr. Palmer said:

> I have said to them – and to their credit be it testified, the proposition has generally been accepted as the council of wisdom – if you are to be a historic people, you must work out your own destiny upon your own

foundation. You gain nothing by a parasitic clinging to the White race; and immeasurably less, by trying to jostle them out of place. If you have no power of development from within, you lack the first quality of a historic race, and must, sooner or later, go to the wall.... Were I a Black man, I should plead for a pure Black race, as, being a White man I claim it for the White race; and should only ask the opportunity for it to work out its mission.... The true policy of both races is, that they shall stand apart in their own social grade, in their own schools, in their own ecclesiastical organizations, under their own teachers and guides: but with all the kindness and helpful co-operations to which the old relations between the races, and their present dependence on each other would naturally predispose.

Morton Howison Smith (1923-) was a professor at Belhaven College in Jackson, Mississippi, and is one of the few remaining founding ministers of the Presbyterian Church in America. He is also Professor Emeritus at Greenville Theological Seminary in South Carolina.

This study appeared in *The Southern Presbyterian Journal*, July 7, 1957, Vol. XVI, No. 10.

XIII

Some Needed Distinctions
by Lamuel Nelson Bell

The mounting racial tensions in some areas are be-clouding the judgment of some good men. Also, there is a confusion of terms which is often adding to tensions.

First: Desegregation and Integration are not synonymous terms.

The writer believes that forced segregation is un-Christian because it denies the rights which are inherent in American citizenship.

We would affirm with equal conviction that forced integration is also un-Christian because it denies other rights also inherent in American citizenship.

To abolish laws which humiliate and discriminate against any citizen is something we believe Christians should work for. To make it equally clear that social equalities are earned and not imposed by law is also consistent with the Christian conscience.

Second: Because a Christian, in good conscience, works for the laying aside of the discriminations and humiliations and restrictions of the past, in so far as they relate to the

Negro, this should not place that Christian outside the pale of Christian fellowship, nor should he be accused of "selling out" to his social heritage of the past or to the theological liberalism of the present.

We believe some of the racial tensions of our day have been caused by ill-advised enthusiasts who have equated desegregation with integration and have looked upon segregated churches as un-Christian and integrated churches as the epitome of brotherly love. Where segregated churches are the result of natural selection and not prejudice, they are far more Christian in spirit than churches which have deliberately espoused a forced or unnatural integration to show how good they are.

We also believe some of the tensions of our day are caused by men who are determined to maintain White supremacy by fear and lawlessness.

It is to Christians, Negro and White, that the world should look for both an example and a solution. Far too little is said about the daily contacts where courtesy, mutual consideration and love should characterize our dealings. In fact, Christian race relations begin in this area.

We all need to consider the feelings of others and put ourselves in their place. Recently the writer was eating in the airport restaurant in Atlanta. Four well-dressed and quiet Negro women came in. For a moment there was hesitation at the door and they were then escorted to a far corner of the restaurant and a screen placed around them after which they were served. White Christian, how would you have felt inside had you been humiliated in that way? This procedure may have been necessary under Georgia law, but what we are considering is the feelings of those who are involved.

Of course there are serious problems involved. In some sections of the South, integration of schools would be folly. Even in Washington, D. C., integration has created such serious problems that the only solution many are finding is the removal of their children from the public school system.

There are other serious problems because some people confuse legal and spiritual rights with social privileges. The first is acquired by birth in our country. The second is the gift of God. The third is something earned, and it cannot be defended as a right nor can it be imposed by law.

We believe entirely too many discussions expend time and energy on theories. What is needed today are practical means of arriving at workable solutions. For the individual Christian this means treating every other person as he himself would want to be treated. For communities this should mean the formation of a group of representatives from both races, under Christian leadership and direction. Let such leaders sit down and talk over the problems involved. We believe the heartaches and tensions in Montgomery could have been avoided by such a conference at the beginning, for the original request of Negro leaders to the bus company was reasonable.

Such conferences will reveal that many Negro leaders are keenly aware of the problems brought about by desegregation and largely prefer that alignments continue on a voluntary segregated basis. The crux of the issue is one of legalized discrimination. Remove this and nine-tenths of the tensions will disappear.

But, where mutual conferences are denied, a far greater

danger lies ahead, for this intransigent attitude opens the door for the extremists on both sides – men who may let prejudice and hate take precedence over mutual consideration and Christian love.

That which we have written may suit very few, but we believe that in this general direction lies the only means of arriving at a Christian solution for a difficult problem.

This editorial appeared in *The Southern Presbyterian Journal*, June 5, 1957, Vol. XVI, No. 6.

XIV

A Southern Christian Looks
at the Race Problem
by Rev. Guy T. Gillespie, D.D., Litt.D.

The charge has been frequently and loudly made that White people of the South are so blinded with prejudice and so filled with enmity against the Negro race that they cannot see the race problem in its true perspective. Personally, and on behalf of some thirty million or more other Southern Christians, I wish to challenge the fairness and truth of that charge.

Prejudice is properly defined as "a judgment or opinion formed without knowledge or due examination of the facts." If any people on the face of the earth have had ample opportunity to learn at first hand the facts about the race problem, unquestionably the Southern people must be accorded the pre-eminence in that respect. For more than two hundred years the two races have lived here side by side, in relatively large numbers, in close and intimate contact, and on terms of mutual understanding and good will, so that out of this experience there has come, not only to the White people, but to the Negro as well, a vast accumulation of knowledge and practical wisdom in meeting the day-to-day problems of personal and race relationships. Moreover, let it be said with all emphasis, in spite of all the hue and cry which has been raised in recent years, we Southern people, as a rule, do not have any enmity or ill-will in our hearts against Negroes, but only feelings of kindliness and genuine sympathy. As friends and neighbors we wish to see them have better homes, higher standards of living, better schools for their children, and the fullest opportunity for development as law-abiding, liberty-loving, self-respecting citizens.

If there is any room therefore for a general charge of race prejudice it would seem to lie not against Southern Christians, but against that very considerable group of sentimental enthusiasts whose knowledge of this problem is limited to what they read in the newspapers and sensational magazines, and to the grossly exaggerated and distorted information furnished to them by self-serving propaganda agencies, and yet who assume that they have all the answers to this difficult and complex problem, and a divine warrant to solve it by remote control.

The Supreme Court Decision

Southern Christians, generally, feel that the Supreme Court decision, outlawing the principle of segregation and ordering integration of the races in the public schools of the nation, was a tragic mistake. This decree reversed previous decisions of the Supreme Court which had served as precedents for all Federal and State courts for more than a half century, nullified the constitutional and statutory provisions of seventeen sovereign States, and prescribed radical and revolutionary changes in the long established customs and social traditions of a large proportion of the people of the United States.

Southern Christians cherish a deep reverence for the Federal Constitution, and they wish to respect the dignity and integrity of our courts, and yet to many of us, this sweeping decision of the highest court in virtually taking over the control and regulation of the schools of the nation seems to be a clear violation of the Constitution itself, and an unwarranted usurpation of powers distinctly reserved to the several States and to the people of local communities.

The reasons assigned by the Supreme Court for its revolutionary decision are not based on legal or moral principles, but on the *ex parte* opinions of psychologists and sociologists, whose knowledge of this particular problem has been clearly shown to be superficial, and whose close affiliation with Socialist and Communistic organizations scarcely qualifies them as safe counselors in formulating the policies which are to shape the education of the children of this great democracy, for generations to come.

Believing as we do, that this decision was based upon false premises, that it is unsound in principle, unrealistic and impracticable, and that its consequences, if generally adopted, would prove disastrous and irreparable, we do not regard it as a proper or final adjudication of the issues involved. We believe that it should be reversed, and we appeal to the sober second judgment of the Court itself, to recognize and correct its error; failing that, we shall continue to appeal to the enlightened judgment and the unfailing common sense of the fair-minded people of the nation to join us in mobilizing public sentiment in support of some wiser and better solution of the problem. For this attitude we have ample encouragement and high precedent. The Supreme Court has often reversed its own decisions, following changes in the personnel of the Court or in the political climate. Abraham Lincoln, in similar opposition to the pronouncement of a Supreme Court of his time, declared: "That burlesque of a judicial decision must be expunged from the books of authority.... We mean to reverse it; and we mean to reverse it peaceably" (See *Lincoln Encyclopedia*, MacMillan, 1950, pp. 88ff). The events proved that Lincoln was no false prophet. Men of like vision and courage, who do not give up because the odds are against them, may live to see history repeat itself in our generation.

The Crux of the Problem

In the South and in urban centers in the North, where the Negro population approximates or exceeds that of the White, enforced integration of the schools, just in proportion as the experiment succeeded, would inevitably lead to the cultivation of such attitudes and social intimacies as would result in intermarriage between the two groups, and eventually to the blurring of all racial distinctions, and the amalgamation of the Negro and White races.

Here therefore is the crux of the whole racial problem: Is it desirable that social relations leading normally to intermarriage and ultimate racial amalgamation should be encouraged and approved; or, is it more desirable, in the interests of all parties and society as a whole, that racial intermarriage should be discouraged or prohibited, and that each race should be enabled to preserve its own racial integrity?

This is the issue which overshadows all other considerations in the minds of parents in typical Southern communities, which explains their uncompromising opposition to the integrated school, and which also explains the traditional Southern attitude with respect to social intermingling of the races in homes, churches, hotels, public assemblies, recreation, transportation and other public facilities.

Many well-meaning civil and religious leaders who now endorse the policy of integration in schools, churches and other areas of life seem to ignore, or deliberately refuse to recognize, that the question of intermarriage and complete racial integration is necessarily involved, and is bound to overshadow all other issues in the minds of people whose children will be forced to serve as guinea pigs in this dangerous experiment in race relations.

To his credit, be it said that the average Southern Negro attaches little importance to the possibility of intermarriage with the White race, and if left to himself would naturally prefer marriage within his own race. For this reason the professional agitators and Negro leaders have had comparatively little to say concerning intermarriage, and have based their appeal on the very natural desire of Negro parents to secure equal educational opportunities for their children, and on the exploitation of some of the (petty) grievances which the Negro feels, by insisting that he is being discriminated against as "a second class citizen."

However, many of the self-appointed promoters of the integration movement are fully aware of the inherent and logical implications of the race-mixing program with re-

spect to intermarriage, and as one of them has frankly
stated, the goal which they seek in America is "a social
democracy which either begins with marriage, or necessarily includes marriage in its ideals and principles."

Segregation From the Southern Viewpoint

After long and painful experience, Southern people are
firmly convinced that where two widely different races live
together in the same area in approximately equal numbers,
that the only alternative to racial amalgamation is some
reasonable and equitable form of segregation.

The pattern of segregation which has been in operation
in the South, and throughout the nation generally, is the
result of a gradual process of evolution for many generations. It must be admitted that it has not always been consistent or equitable, and some of its features cannot be defended on rational or ethical grounds. Like all human institutions, it is still far from perfect. On the whole, however,
it has provided a working basis for mutual understanding
and effective co-operation between the two races. With
occasional exceptions, peace and order have been preserved, mutual confidence and goodwill have been fos-
tered, and each race has been able in the main to preserve
its racial integrity, and to develop cultural and social patterns suited to its own capacities and needs.

The evils and injustices which have arisen under the
system of segregation have been purely incidental, and
have not been due to any fallacy in the principle of segregation, but to the weaknesses and perversities of individual
members of both races. Southern Christians do not con-
done these wrongs, but everywhere condemn them, and

are anxious to see them corrected. Up until the recent violent agitation precipitated by the Supreme Court decisions, steady progress was being made in the correction of such abuses and unfair practices and in the improvement of race relations. Even yet, except in a few localities, there is no indication of any serious disturbance of the friendly relations existing between the rank and file of Negroes and Whites throughout the South; which is a tribute not only to the good sense and self restraint of both groups, but also to the basic soundness and practicality of the system of segregation under which they have lived and worked.

Recognizing, therefore, that the system of segregation as heretofore maintained has certain obvious defects, but believing that in the course of time these objectionable features may be eliminated without sacrificing the major objective, we Southern Christians, with some exceptions chiefly in the border States, approve the determination of our civil leaders to employ every legal expedient to prevent the integration of our schools, and to preserve the principle of segregation as a permanent feature of our public policy, with the confident assurance that in the long run, it will prove best for the present and the future welfare of both races.

The Moral and Ethical Basis for Segregation

Aside from all questions of expediency, of constitutional technicalities, or of local interests, there is a firm conviction in the minds of Southern people that the principle of segregation is amply supported by scientific, historical and biblical data, and that it may be defended on moral and ethical grounds, and as consistent with the principles of Christianity and the great traditions of American democracy. The limits of this discussion will permit only a brief summary of several of these reasons, which are believed to be factual and logical.

1. The widely different characteristics of the White and Negro races would render complete integration illogical and impracticable.

Modern anthropologists have discarded the term *race* as applicable to separate groups of people. They contend the differences shade off so gradually within each group, that no valid distinction can be made between the groups. Their contention, however, appears to be largely a war about words or definitions. Actually, as a matter of common observation, we know that there are broad lines of difference between the several major branches of the human family, and whether they are properly called races or by some other designation, the White, the Yellow, the Brown, and the Black groups each have their own distinctive physical and cultural characteristics. For all practical purposes, therefore, we may just as well follow common usage, and refer to them as separate races.

Between the White and Negro races, with which we are directly concerned, these differences are quite obvious, not only as to the pigment of the skin, but many other physical features. Even greater and more important than these physical differences, are those which relate to mental, emotional, and moral development, esthetic appreciation, social and religious impulses and experiences. It is not necessary to ask or determine whether one of these races is superior to the other; for, after all, that is only an academic question, and the decision would depend upon the standard of measurement and the qualities which were measured. One race is likely to rate high on one point and low on others, and vice versa. Of one thing, however, there is abundant and indisputable evidence – these two races differ in a great many respects. These differences are not incidental or superficial; they are fundamental, and any failure to recognize this fact is bound to generate irritations and tensions resulting in individual and social disorders and the ultimate impairment or destruction of moral and cultural values. That such racial differences have a decisive bearing on the problem of race relations, and that they constitute a valid reason for the separation of the White and Negro races, is corroborated by no less an authority on race problems than President Lincoln, who, in a speech to a group of free Negroes at the White House in 1862, said: "You and we are different races. Whether it is right or wrong, I need not discuss, but this physical difference is a great disadvantage to us both, as I think... it affords a reason at least why we should be separated."

2. Intermarriage between widely different racial groups is unnatural, unfair to offspring, and prejudicial to human progress.

In all nature God has endowed His living creatures with an instinct to mate only with their own kind. The old adage, "Birds of a feather flock together," only expresses a universal law of nature. Bluebirds never mate with redbirds, doves with blackbirds, or mocking birds with jays. The intelligent farmer does not allow his dairy and beef breeding stock to run in the same pasture; otherwise he would down-grade his herds, and have only a herd of scrubs or mongrels. The same principle applies with even

greater force to the mating of human beings of widely different types and cultural backgrounds. The offspring are
generally unstable, eccentric, ill-adjusted, unpredictable,
and unhappy. Extend the experiment on a large scale and
over successive generations, and the result is a retarded or
decadent civilization. Both science and history confirm the
truth that progress for the human species as well as for the
lower orders of nature comes through selective breeding
rather than through mongrelization.

Lebon, the noted French psychologist and sociologist
of the past century, testifies as follows:

> It is an historical fact that human stocks that have
> produced the highest civilizations have been strains of
> stock without mixture for many generations. Every race
> of fixed type that has attained the highest civilization,
> has quickly lost its power and standing after mixing with
> another race radically different.

In confirmation of the truth of this observation we
have but to cite the remarkable virility of the cultures of the
Hebrews, the Greeks, and the English speaking peoples, all
of whom kept their racial stocks pure, as contrasted with
the retarded or decadent civilizations of India, Egypt,
Spain, Portugal, who allowed their racial stocks to become
mixed with the diverse peoples with whom they came in
contact. Or, to take an illustration closer to home; compare
the achievements and progress of the people of North
America, including Negroes as well as White people,
where the principle of racial segregation has been generally
maintained, with the status of the peoples of Central and
South America where there is no color line, since the set-

tlers from the Latin Nations of Europe freely intermarried with the native Indians and imported Negro slaves. Let those who now so strongly urge the integration of White and colored races in this country cross the Rio Grande, and travel all the way to the southern tip of South America, and see the ignorance, poverty, squalor, superstition, undeveloped resources, inefficient and unstable governments, frequent revolutions, ruthless dictatorships, and the many other evidences of the blight that results from the mixing of dissimilar races!

To the same effect is the testimony of the late Dr. Charles W. Eliot, President of Harvard University, who with a staff of experts was sent by the Carnegie Foundation for Peace, to study the effect of race mixtures in the Orient. After spending many months in China, India, Japan, and the islands of the Pacific, they submitted their report, the gist of which is as follows:

> First: The experience of the East teaches that the intermarriage of races which are distinctly unlike is undesirable because the progeny of such mixtures are, as a rule, inferior to each of the parent stocks, both physically and morally; a fact which has been demonstrated in large scale. Second: The Orient teaches the world that the pure race is best, and the crosses between unlike races seldom turn out well.

In the light of these indisputable facts, how can we consider any proposal or policy which involves the gradual integration and ultimate amalgamation of the White and colored races in the United States, except as a colossal blunder, a betrayal of unborn generations and a monstrous crime against civilization?

3. The principle of segregation is in harmony with the purpose and will of God as revealed in His Word, and is consistent with the teachings and spirit of our Lord Jesus Christ.

God Himself thwarted the first man-made plan of integration, by the confusion of tongues at the Tower of Babel, and scattered the peoples abroad upon the face of the whole earth. Whether one accepts that as a true story, as do most Southern Christians, or whether the allegorical interpretation of modern liberal scholarship is preferred, the fact remains that divine Providence is directly responsible for the linguistic differences and other factors which have served to keep the peoples of the earth segregated into tribal, national or racial groups, from prehistoric times down to our day. By special divine decree Abraham and his descendants were separated from all the other peoples of the earth, and for fifteen hundred years Israel existed as a strictly segregated nation. They were forbidden by God to mingle socially, to intermarry, or to amalgamate with the nations around them. Violations of this command were considered as a capital offense, and punished with great severity, by Moses and later by Ezra.

Jesus used the Parable of the Good Samaritan to rebuke the smug complacency and narrow minded intolerance of the Jews and to show that the duty to love our neighbors is a practical principle of sympathy and helpfulness which knows no limitation of nationality or race. At the same time He did not ignore or denounce racial distinctions, nor did He set plans on foot to abolish them or to bring about amalgamation of the Jews with the Samaritans or other races. Insofar as we have any record, there is no indication that Jesus or the Apostles were ever called upon to pass judgment upon the question of the rightness or wrongness of racial segregation or racial integration; certainly no question was raised concerning the mixing of races as dissimilar as the White and Negro races. Since this is primarily and essentially a social or political question, and since our Lord on several occasions refused to decide controversial issues of a social or political nature, but left these matters to the reason and conscience of the individual, we are justified in concluding that He has given us no mandate on this matter, but has left us free to decide the question in the light of reason and experience and the broad principles set forth in the Old as well as in the New Testament.

In this connection, therefore, and by way of reply to the statements made recently by numerous church leaders and various ecclesiastical bodies denouncing segregation as "unjust," "sinful," "wicked," "displeasing to God" and "essentially un-Christian," from our point of view we confidently affirm; First: Since the practice of segregation was instituted among the Hebrew people by divine authority, and enforced by stern theocratic sanctions for many centuries, and since Christ and the Apostles demonstrated that the principles of charity and Christian brotherhood could be made operative in all the relations of life without involving revolutionary changes in the social, economic, or political order, there is certainly no valid ground for the charge that segregation is inherently wrong, contrary to the will of God, and essentially un-Christian.

4. Segregation is a well-considered and time-tested American policy, and, is consistent with the principles of

true Americanism.

Ample evidence is available to show that segregation is in accord with the best thinking of representative American leadership, and as a time-tested American policy, rests upon moral and ethical principles, and not upon blind and unreasoning prejudice, as has been loudly charged by some of its latter-day critics.

Seventeen of the States of the Union have incorporated the principle of segregation into their constitutions. Most of the other States have approved it by statutory provisions, and all of the States, with one or two exceptions, at one time or another, have adopted laws prohibiting interracial marriages. State and Federal courts have uniformly approved these constitutional and statutory provisions, and until the violent political agitation was started some years ago, segregation was generally accepted as a firmly established principle of American public policy.

Thomas Jefferson, author of the Declaration of Independence, and Abraham Lincoln, author of the Emancipation Proclamation, both strongly opposed to the institution of slavery, were both so completely convinced of the necessity of the segregation of the races that they earnestly advocated the repatriation of the Negroes to Africa or the West Indies. Since the abolition of slavery, many representative leaders in Church and State, both in the North and in the South, who felt a keen sympathy for the Negro and wished to help him improve his lot, never questioned or proposed but that this should be done, and could be done, within the framework of a segregated society.

It was the recognition of this truth as an essential feature of the American way of life, which made Booker T.

Washington an influential national leader and the greatest benefactor of the Negro race in the past generation. All would-be leaders and promoters of better race relations in America today would do well to study his realistic approach to the problem and follow his able and far-seeing Christian leadership. In a notable and epoch-making address delivered at the Atlanta Exposition in 1895, pleading for understanding and co-operation between the races, he held aloft the torch which must guide us to the ultimate solution of this great and pressing problem. It is eminently fitting therefore that this discussion should be concluded with a quotation of his wise words. He said:

> The wisest among my race understand that agitation of questions of social equality is the extremest folly, and that progress in the enjoyment of all the privileges that will come to us must be the result of severe and constant struggle rather than of artificial forcing.... In all things that are purely social, we can be separate as the fingers, yet one as the hand in all things essential to mutual progress.

Guy T. Gillespie (1884-1958) was a minister in the PCUS and President Emeritus at Belhaven College, Jackson, Mississippi.

This editorial appeared in *The Southern Presbyterian Journal*, June 5, 1957, Vol. XVI, No. 6.

www.ingramcontent.com/pod-product-compliance
Lightning Source LLC
Chambersburg PA
CBHW071416090426
42737CB00011B/1482